TO

HIGH
FREQUENCY
CHANGE

WHY WE FEEL LIKE CHANGE
HAPPENS FASTER NOW,
AND WHAT TO DO ABOUT IT

Be more athletic!

Tom

Published by
LID Publishing Limited
The Record Hall, Studio 204,
16-16a Baldwins Gardens,
London EC1N 7RJ, UK

524 Broadway, 11th Floor, Suite 08-120,
New York, NY 10012, US

info@lidpublishing.com
www.lidpublishing.com

A member of:

BPR
Business Publishers Roundtable

www.businesspublishersroundtable.com

Printed in Great Britain by TJ International
ISBN: 978-1-912555-22-2

Cover and page design: Caroline Li

TOM CHEESEWRIGHT

HIGH FREQUENCY CHANGE

WHY WE FEEL LIKE CHANGE HAPPENS FASTER NOW, AND WHAT TO DO ABOUT IT

MADRID | MEXICO CITY | LONDON
NEW YORK | BUENOS AIRES
BOGOTA | SHANGHAI | NEW DELHI

CONTENTS

....

PART 1
HOW CHANGE HAS CHANGED
14

....

ACKNOWLEDGMENTS

Thanks to the clients who've given me access to so many different industries over the last few years. Without you, futurism would still be a hobby.

Thanks to Mum and Dad for inspiration and motivation, to Isabelle and Sophie for love and laughs, and to Monika, for being the one who even then believed.

HORSE-SIZED DUCKS

"Would you rather fight a horse-sized duck or a hundred duck-sized horses?"

This must count as among the more unusual questions asked to a sitting President, but asked it was during a Reddit 'Ask Me Anything' session in 2012. President Obama did not have an answer.

This question first appeared as a letter to the UK's *Metro* newspaper back in 2003. Since then versions of it have become a recurring internet meme. It may sound like a late-night topic for a bunch of stoners, and that is probably where it came from, but I think it captures the challenge facing us all right now rather well.

Neither of the options is particularly attractive. The only reasonable answer I can find is that I would choose to fight the foe I am most 'prepared' to tackle. If I have encountered a big, quacking beast before, then I would at least be more prepared to take it on. I might even have a large supply of pancakes and plum sauce ready. And if I have never faced a whinnying horde of knee-high colts then it is going to be quite the shock as they gallop around, nipping at my ankles. If I had prepared for one and had to face the other, I would almost certainly lose.

In this book I will argue that we are all trained and equipped, as individuals and as organizations, to fight the equivalent of a horse-sized duck: change that is large scale but slow moving. Today we are facing a hundred duck-sized horses, smaller but still disruptive, and very fast-moving waves of change. And we are losing.

LIFE IN FAST FORWARD

Do you ever feel like you want a pause button for the world? Like things just move too damned fast? Do you sometimes feel as though your head is spinning? You have barely got your head around one thing when the next big thing comes along?

If you do, then you are not alone. At the start of many of the talks I give, I ask the audience if they feel like change happens faster now. I'm not specific about the type of change or where it is happening, whether at home or at work. The line between the two is so often blurred now that I'm not sure it matters. No one ever asks me to clarify, but they feel it. Around 80-90% of the audience rapidly raise their hands. There is a widely-shared sense that the pace of change has accelerated, and it goes beyond the inevitable effect of age. The older we are, the more time seems to fly by, but as I shall explain, this sense is shared by people from their twenties to their seventies.

Whether you personally feel it or not, something fundamental has changed over recent years that has made it harder to keep pace with events. Whether or not the overall rate of change has accelerated is one of the main subjects of this book. You can read on to find my conclusion. But something is happening, and it is causing deeper problems than just leaving some of us with our heads spinning.

For us, as individuals, there is a challenge to our work and our careers. Can we adapt with enough speed or will we be left behind? Will our skills and knowledge become out of date and ill-suited to a job market that has moved on? For organizations, this is an existential threat. If the competition adapts fast and you fail, then even the largest and most powerful brands can be brought low, as recent experiences have shown.

This book attempts to explain the sense of acceleration that so many of us feel, and the shift in reality that has brought down so many major organizations. Is change really happening faster now? There are good arguments against this idea that this book will explore. In Part One, I hope to make you think differently about the nature of change and how we understand it.

That done, this book turns to the practical: how do you respond to a world of 'high frequency change'? I cannot promise this book will stop your head spinning. I'm not a psychologist, a therapist or a meditation guru. This book will not prescribe yoga or walks in nature to help you reconnect with a slower pace of life. What it will do is offer practical advice about how to build a career that is, to some extent, insulated from constant change. And about how to build a business that can adapt more easily to the new environment.

TIME AND AGE

For a time, I used to think that the sense of acceleration people reported to me was just down to the type of people I tend to talk to in my role as an applied futurist. Specifically, I thought it might be a factor of their age.

In my role I mostly spend my time working with senior executives in large organizations to answer three questions:

- What does our future look like?
- How do we tell that story to our colleagues, customers, partners and stakeholders?
- What do we do next?

The leaders and executives I work with and speak to tend to be in their forties. As someone who has just entered their forties, I'm pleased to say this is still young by modern standards, but there is no doubt that the perception of time speeds up as you age. Each second is simply a smaller fraction of our total life than it was. We repeat more things in a natural and necessary routine to get through our complex lives. There is less chance for reflection and fewer milestones for our memory to latch on to. And many of us are trying to keep up with the change in our children's lives at the same time as our own. These are all well-established ideas that might explain some of the sense of acceleration as we age.

What convinced me that this did not explain the reported sense of acceleration were conversations with younger cohorts and the people who work with them.

I found people in their late teens questioning the value of their university education, clear in the understanding that whatever they learned on their particular vocational course, whether it was digital marketing, management or computer science, would be out of date by the time they reached the workplace. Moreover, I spoke to academics who acknowledged that some of their fields were moving so fast as to be almost unteachable. One went so far as to say that their discipline could not and should not be taught in a traditional sense, at least not on a three-year under-graduate programme.

The current sense that we are living in an accelerated time goes beyond the normal complaints of age. It is affect-ing the young (in their forties) and the younger, and cer-tainly those no longer technically young.

THE EXISTENTIAL THREAT

A sense of acceleration is one thing, but it was its effects that convinced me of the value of trying to understand it, not least in the spate of high-profile business failures; companies with strong balance sheets and loyal customer bases, who lost both because they were left behind by trends. How could this happen? How could a company that had survived and even thrived for decades be so suddenly wrong-footed?

What I came to recognize is that most businesses are built to adapt to a particular type of change. This type of change has allowed them long periods in which they could operate successfully on fundamentally the same model; long periods during which they had the luxury to focus on optimization, not adaptation. The result was that they had become increasingly good – by which I usually mean 'efficient' – at doing what they did. But, at the same time, they had become less capable of spotting the need for change. They had failed to recognize the moment when what they did was no longer the right thing to do. Years of investment sunk into doing one thing well made it incredibly hard to choose to do something different when the time came.

Put simply, we, as a business culture, have spent decades learning how to optimize at the expense of agility. I will argue that in an age of high frequency change, agility trumps optimization as a predictor of sustainable success. The best businesses are now places of constant experimentation.

They can accommodate rapid expansion but also rapid contraction. They know how to recognize failure, accept it and learn from it with minimal cost and pain. They accept uncertainty and expose themselves to it in order to learn. The tools of business that we have relied on for years are no longer fit for purpose. We need a new way of doing things that is fit for the future.

A TOOLKIT FOR AGILE ORGANIZATIONS

What might a new way of doing things look like? If you accept the argument for high frequency change over the next few chapters, then you will also recognize that the timescales which our businesses have been built on are no longer correct. Fundamentally, business planning is built on two different time frames: short term and long term. The short term ranges from a quarter to a year, depending on your regulatory constrictions and listing requirements. It is primarily financial, and it is tied to returning shareholder or stakeholder value within those time brackets.

Long-term planning tends to be over five years, with the expectation that structural changes to the market happen infrequently and can, in some way, be planned for. There is very little solid, strategic planning over the medium term that is not explicitly based on the prospect of business as usual. In my experience, most strategic change in this time window is driven almost exclusively by external events:

change in the medium term is enforced and reactive. What proactive planning there is rarely takes account of what is happening beyond the bounds of the business or the immediate industry.

A more agile organization recognizes that it needs to change more frequently at a more fundamental level. It sets up systems for scanning the near horizon for opportunities and obstacles. It accelerates the process of strategic decision-making. And it structures itself to be able to act on those strategic revisions.

These three principles: enhanced senses, accelerated decision-making and organizational agility form the principles for Athletic Organizations and are laid out in more detail in Part Two of this book.

BEING FUTURE-READY

This idea of Athletic Organizations offers a recipe for businesses, charities and public bodies. But what about the people working in them? There is an undoubted threat to employment from the rise of machines. Augmented by machines, fewer people can do more. While this does not mean there will not be work – and new forms of work – in the future, the demands are likely to be different as large numbers of current jobs are naturally replaced by more profitable machines.

How do you build or develop a career that is in some way insulated from this threat? What do you teach your children or your young employees today to give them the best chance in the future?

The answer comes from understanding both the nature of tomorrow's high frequency world, and the skills that are harder, more expensive or, for now at least, impossible for machines to replicate; uniquely human capabilities that will allow people to carve out a successful career in tomorrow's world of work.

I loosely refer to the critical skills for tomorrow's workforce as 'The Three Cs': the ability to curate, create and communicate. You can read about these skills, why they are so important, and how to develop them, in Part Three of this book.

WHAT'S NEXT?

One would have to have an ego of magnificent proportions to believe they could cram a complete prescription for tomorrow's world into a single volume. Understanding and responding to high frequency change is a critical step for sustainable success in both the personal and corporate domains. But it is not the only thing to understand.

The motivating force that is enabling and driving high frequency change has other effects too. The low friction environment enabled by technology is also supporting a more diverse environment than ever before with endless choice and endless competition. The amplification of human power has its own distinct effects that require explanation, as does the accelerated speed at which we increasingly operate on a day-to-day basis and the rise in expectations this brings. Low friction has enabled the rapid reshaping of our organizations, public and private, and has helped to define a new architecture for tomorrow's cities, corporations and personal relations.

These are ideas that I continue to explore on my blog and that I hope to one day turn into books in their own right.

But for now, let us stick with this book. And the first thing to do is explain how we have moved from an age of horse-sized ducks to one of duck-sized horses ...

PART 1

HOW CHANGE HAS CHANGED

CHAPTER 1

HISTORY'S GRAND ARC

Is the world spinning faster now? Does change really happen at a greater rate now than it did in the past? There are two sides in this debate: the accelerationists and the historians. It is hardly the Mods and the Rockers, but it is nonetheless an interesting clash of cultures.

The accelerationist movement arguably started on the west coast of the US and in Silicon Valley. Its most famous prophet is Ray Kurzweil, Google's chief futurist. Accelerationists believe we are heading towards some form of change crescendo, 'the Singularity'. They argue that the rate of change has been accelerating constantly over the last few thousand years, driven by technologies that amplify our powers and shrink our world. They point to Moore's law, the recognition by one of the co-founders of Intel that the number of transistors you can economically fit on a silicon chip doubles every couple of years and has done so since the 1960s. What this mouthful means for us is exponential increases in the bang for buck we can expect from our digital machines. That performance has knock-on effects: accelerating financial transactions, medical research and the spread of ideas in general. Ultimately, the accelerationists believe technology takes over. Artificial intelligence becomes capable of evolving its own design and influencing, if not controlling, every aspect of our world. With machines able to iterate and innovate at the speed of light, the rate of change rises off the charts. They believe that the sense of acceleration we feel today is just the precursor to this dramatic transformation.

Historians say that, frankly, this is bollocks. They challenge our sense of acceleration and suggest that people have always felt this way. The world is always changing, and we always struggle to keep up. Historians point to periods of incredible change over the last couple of centuries and question whether our current connected computing revolution stacks up against major events from history, like the Industrial Revolution.[1]

I challenge both of these perspectives, because they both rely on a central idea that seems to me to be obviously wrong: that change is something that can be measured in a single dimension. Can we really consider the grand arc of history in terms as simple as 'fast' and 'slow'? History books do not have a speedometer on them. Reality is much more complex than this.

Of course, when things are extremely complex we tend, as a species, to turn to heuristics, a posh word for rules of thumb that help us to understand things. Maybe we do need a heuristic to help us understand the pace of change; it just needs to be a little more involved than simply 'fast' or 'slow'. To get to one, let us consider some of the examples of accelerated change we see today and some from the past.

SPIN CYCLE

The washing machine might be the most revolutionary piece of technology of the last two centuries. Just look at the scale of its impact: global, social, economic, political, cultural. The washing machine reshaped houses and households, supported women's liberation,[2] enabled the explosion of the leisure industry and, perhaps not so positively, fast fashion.

Don't believe me? In 1953, Britons would spend an average of 63 hours per week on housework.[3] And when I say Britons, let us be clear: most of that burden was shouldered by women. By 1965, according to a separate study, this had dropped to 44 hours per week.[4] Today, the average is somewhere between two and eighteen hours per week, depending on which study you believe, or whether you have the walking muck-cyclones that are young children.

If you are working 63 hours a week just to keep the house running, then the prospects of a career are remote, as is the chance of leisure time, unless you really enjoy washing, ironing and cleaning. By automating one of the most time-consuming and energy-sapping tasks of running a household, the washing machine and its mechanical siblings changed our lives in the most dramatic ways.

But this transformation took time. The mass adoption of domestic automation appliances began in the 1920s in the US and the 1950s in Europe, but it took a long time for them to reach the majority of households. This was a change of enormous magnitude but at relatively slow speed.

UNEMPLOYED HORSES

At the end of the 19th century, nearly a million horses were still employed on farms across Great Britain.[5] Though commercial steam engines had been available for nearly 200 years, and cheaper portable engines for over 50,[6] horses remained a popular form of motive power. Specially-bred working horses pulled ploughs and turned mills. And they were not just employed on the farms. Millions more dragged slate and coal from mines and drew carts through towns. Horses remained a defining part of rural and urban landscapes, and were the basis of much employment. All those horses needed handling, feeding, caring for. A few million horses provided work for perhaps as many people.

Then came the motor vehicle. For a long time the rail industry successfully lobbied to limit the success of the car industry. The 1865 'Red Flag Act' restricted the speed of motor vehicles to 4mph in the countryside and just 2mph in towns, and required any vehicle drawing multiple wagons to have a man carrying a red flag walk out in front. Even three decades later, at the end of the century, the speed limit was only lifted to 14mph.

However, none of this prevented the inevitable. By the time of the First World War, the combustion engine was taking over. Farm machinery was switching from one horse to many horsepower. Cars – many still steam-powered – were replacing carriages. And on the battlefield, the combustion engine was beginning to change the shape of warfare, powering the first tanks and accelerating supply lines.

Inevitably, war-time investment accelerated the development of the combustion engine. In the inter-war period, petrol overtook steam as the preferred form of propulsion for personal transport. Cars like the Austin 7 sold in their hundreds of thousands, while across the pond the Ford Model A sold millions. By the 1930s, recognizably modern vehicles had started to appear: the Volkswagen Beetle and the Citröen Traction Avant. We were truly in the age of the motor car.

By the Second World War even the conservative cavalry had relinquished their horses. Millions of horses joined the equine unemployment line, and many came to a very sticky end.

Think about the scale of change this represented – not just for the horses. Think about it in terms of your senses: the switch from horses to cars changed the way the world looked, sounded and smelled. It changed the speed and sensation of travel. Think about it in terms of employment: huge numbers of new jobs were created and old ones destroyed, along with large parts of the industries that supported them. Coach builders, still so-called today, became car-customizers or faced collapse. Farmers could mechanize or be overwhelmed by the productivity increases of their neighbours. Think about it in terms of lifestyle: places that were uncomfortably reachable in a day became easy trips in a couple of hours. Families could be more distributed and remain connected. Cars changed the way we live and work, reshaping our cities and our countryside.

This change took decades, but it completely changed all our lives.

THE JETSET

War also shaped another critical change of the 20th century: the jet aircraft. Following the rapidly accelerated development of the jet for military purposes, domestic use began in peace time. But it took a few years before it became a reliable form of transport, and even more before it became widely affordable and had its great impact.

The power of the jet aircraft is to shrink the world, to bring distant places closer and allow the more rapid movement of people, products and ideas. Jet aircraft typically cruise at least 25% faster than their prop-driven counterparts. They are more efficient at high speed and high altitude, making larger aircraft and longer journeys more affordable. Only with the jet engine could we conceive of cost-effective business trips and budget package holidays.

Of course, these were not the first civilian uses. Air travel was a luxury enjoyed by the wealthy, with 'the Jetset' flying to London, Paris or New York for swanky parties. Transatlantic flights would cost thousands, domestic flights across the US twice as much as they do now.[7] Before the jet aircraft there were no express package services that could deliver over long distances. Air freight was inordinately expensive.

Before the use of any of these services could expand, and prices could fall, the aircraft had to be safe and reliable, and the first ... were not. The De Haviland Comet, the first jet airliner, suffered from serious structural issues with some early models breaking up in flight due to metal fatigue.

It took years of revisions and redesigns before the model reached something close to modern safety standards.

The jet aircraft has shrunk our world and allowed more of us to see more of it, but getting to that point took time – decades. Another slow speed change of great magnitude.

CHAPTER 2

HYPER CYCLE

The story of the hoverboard is a surprising illustration of just how much culture, consumerism and commerce have changed in the 21st century. The hoverboard, balance board or 'swegway' (also a brand name), was brought to most people's attention in the spring of 2015 via the TV appearances and Instagram posts of a whole host of celebrities who latched onto the devices quickly or were paid to do so by so-called 'influencer marketing' companies. They began to share videos of themselves riding them around dressing rooms, airports and even on stage. Justin Bieber, Chris Brown, Kendall Jenner. People with millions of followers. Everyone wanted to know: "Where can I get a hoverboard?"

When these devices first made it to the UK, they were expensive. Patent and licensing issues were still being debated.[8] Production volumes were still relatively small, leading to waiting lists. If you wanted to be like Bieber, it was going to set you back somewhere north of £1,500.

The devices were, of course, manufactured in China, specifically Shenzhen. Manufacturers here take a rather more laissez-faire attitude to intellectual property rights. And so many new factories rapidly sprang up making clones of the original hoverboards or, more often, re-tooled from what they were making before. The result? Prices crashed. Online stores sprang up to meet demand. Importers ramped up.

By summer 2015 there was an absolute frenzy of excitement about the devices. Prices crashed as volumes rose, from thousands of pounds to just hundreds. Now you could find hoverboards on the high street, on market stalls and under the feet of children, not just wealthy adults. Everyone seemed to want a hoverboard.

This frenzy reached fever pitch in September 2015. Every news channel and paper seemed to be running the same feature on the phenomenon. The hoverboard was going to be the Christmas hit, resulting in many a stretched stocking at the foot of beds across the country on Christmas morning.

And then, even quicker than it had begun, the phenomenon was over.

Two things happened. First, the UK's Department for Transport clarified guidance on where you could ride a hoverboard.[9] The answer? Unless you were part of the landed gentry, just about nowhere. Because they have motors but no pedals, the hoverboard is classed as motor transport under UK law, and regulated as such. Since it obviously does not meet any of the required standards for cars, there was literally no certification process that would allow you to ride these devices in parks, on pavements or on roads. Suddenly their potential as children's toys or hipster commuter transport evaporated.

Second, hoverboards started exploding. As many more manufacturers had jumped into the market, they had begun to cut corners on component quality as they sought to bring down the price. Batteries and charge controllers were particularly risky components to cut back on, since lithium-ion batteries are prone to thermal runaway. There were fires. Houses burned down.

Just six months after the hoverboard emerged into the public consciousness, and just three since the height of the hype, the product was all but dead. Killed off by a combination of excessive regulation of its use and insufficient regulation in its production.

As you might expect, this failure had a dramatic impact on the companies that had built their business on this phenomenon continuing.[10] Small manufacturers in China, who had tooled up to produce them suddenly, found no demand. In fact, demand dropped off so sharply that these small, often family-owned factories had little chance to transition to new products. Importers who had containers full of the devices in transit found they might not be able to move them on, and if they could, it would be at a heavy discount. Some people had even set up servicing companies to maintain and repair devices that were now coming down to disposable prices, with owners who were much less invested in their maintenance.

The impact was limited to this small corner of industry, but within it, that impact was devastating.

GOING VIRAL

This six-month hype cycle – a 'hyper cycle', if you like – is dramatic but we can see that in general across our shrinking world, products reach larger audiences much faster now than ever before, and they can be displaced just as quickly.

Look at the history of communications technology as an example. The landline telephone took 35 years to reach a quarter of the US population. The mobile phone took just 13 years, and the smartphone around half that time.[11] Whatever replaces the smartphone – my bet is on some form of worn mixed reality device becoming popular in the mid-2020s – will likely spread in twice as fast the time again.

This is an incredible contraction over the last hundred or so years. But the accelerated design, distribution and dismissal of physical products is nothing next to the near-instant spread of digital ideas and services. Facebook took two years to reach 50 million users. Instagram took 19 months to reach 50 million users. Pokémon Go took just 19 days to hit the same milestone.[12]

These are companies with nearly no infrastructure and very few staff developing hugely disruptive products and services that have climbed to prominence at an incredible rate. How disruptive? Facebook, for many brands and media properties, is now the primary channel of communication to their customers. Facebook is firmly embedded in the Forbes Global 500 largest companies. But Pokémon Go? Is it really that disruptive? Consider this: Pokémon Go got 65 million people around the world playing together and made nearly a billion dollars of revenue, all in its first year. That is a billion dollars that is not going elsewhere: on other games, traditional media or sweets from the corner shop. As Netflix acknowledged in a 2019 letter to investors,[13] the competition is now for peoples' time, not between players in the same categories. If you can capture that many peoples' eyeballs and convince them to spend money with you rather than elsewhere, your impact can be very far-reaching.

RISE AND FALL

Companies' fortunes rise and fall based on the success or failure of their products. Perhaps that is why we have seen the turnover of successful companies increase.

Take those featuring in the Standard & Poor's 500 (S&P500), a listing of the largest public companies in the United States, as an example. In the 1960s companies in the S&P500 would typically spend 60 years in this position. That is, if you took a snapshot of all the companies in the list on a particular date and averaged the total amount of time each spent in the list, it would be about 60 years.[14]

Do the same exercise today and the average is just 15-20 years. The time companies spend in the S&P500 has fallen by a factor of three or four over the course of 60 years. Why? Part of the answer is increased activity in mergers and acquisitions: names disappear because they are swallowed up. Part of it is the natural cycle of disruption: we have always lost big names when they fail to keep pace with change. But this dramatic change in the survival rate of these companies in the listings of the largest has to be, for me, driven in part by this shift in the nature of change. What we are seeing is a higher frequency of change in the names of the businesses and brands that define our lives.

Is this shift replicated among smaller companies? You could cherry-pick figures to say 'yes': in 2008, in the wake of the financial crash, the number of start-up failures in the US overtook the number of new businesses started. But what drove this was not a dramatic increase in the rate of business closures – at least not by historical standards. The closure rate has typically hovered between 8% and 10% for the past 40 years.[15] What drove it is a collapse in the number of new start-ups. Surely in this age of fast-spreading ideas and products, we would expect to see more start-ups rather than fewer?

Commentators point to the US's ageing population to explain this decline and this makes sense when you look at start-ups with a more global perspective. Map the Global Entrepreneurship Index's figures[16] for Total Entrepreneurial Activity (TEA) against the list of the countries with the youngest populations and you see entrepreneurship rates 2-3 times those of the US. In this shrunken world, we must take a global perspective on change and its drivers. Disruptors are not always coming from the expected direction.

SYMPTOMS OF UNCERTAINTY

This accelerated turnover of businesses, driven by the rapid rise and fall of products and services, is visible in more practical aspects of business as well.

If you are sceptical about the idea of a faster-moving, more uncertain business environment, just speak to a manufacturer. One of the best pieces of anecdotal evidence for an accelerating commercial world comes from order sizes. In an uncertain world that is changing fast, companies do not want to gamble on big orders, instead preferring smaller, more frequent deliveries from their suppliers.

A few years ago, at an event where I was speaking, two very successful but completely different manufacturing firms reported that their customers were asking for faster turnaround times on smaller volumes. Holding large amounts of stock has always been problematic for businesses. While it gives you – and perhaps your downstream customers – reassurance, it ties up capital and requires you to operate a larger warehouse yourself.

Practices like Just in Time (JIT) were designed to eliminate a lot of excess stock, freeing capital and reducing operating costs. But while they had the cash and the certainty, lots of companies continued to hold large amounts of product in their warehouses. The alternative was more challenging: capital investment in the skills and systems to manage a leaner process. This is risky. Just look at how many large IT projects fail. Screw this up and you could have catastrophic customer service issues. So, companies put off the investment, preferring the certainty of higher stock levels.

That is until recently. Because, while debt remains relatively cheap for those who can get it, certainty has been eliminated. Now companies are doing anything that they can to minimize the consequences of a misstep, increasing the frequency of deliveries but dropping order sizes, a phenomenon I saw working with a large logistics client.

This client provided consumables to many of the major supermarkets – everything from the blades for the meat slicer on the deli counter, to the tabards the staff wore, to cleaning supplies, to carrier bags. These items are often awkwardly shaped and sized, and shipped irregularly and in small volumes compared to the fast-moving and constant goods supply chain that the supermarkets operate themselves. Nonetheless, the company was having to manage a shift in demand from regular large orders delivered by truck, where all these items were grouped together, to more frequent, smaller orders, delivered by van. We even considered whether they could use Uber or another taxi network to give them more flexibility and speed, given the direction the trend was going.

HEDGING AGAINST UNCERTAINTY

Efforts by companies to protect themselves against this more rapid change manifest as smaller and more frequent orders,perhaps made possible by improved technology. But they also manifest as changes to employment practices, the increasing use of freelancers and the rise of the zero-hours contract. These are the ultimate hedge against uncertainty: resource on tap without the risk of costs when demand diminishes.

At the turn of the century, about 200,000 workers in the UK were on contracts with no guaranteed minimum hours. By 2017 that had risen to about 900,000.[17] In the same period the proportion of self-employed workers in the UK rose from 12% to 15%. The picture elsewhere is similar. In the US some estimates of the freelance workforce rise are as high as 34% of all workers, using perhaps a broader definition of what constitutes freelancing: anyone who has taken on temporary, contract or project-based work.[18] The same report estimates that over half of the US workforce could be self-employed in a few years. Freelancers represent the fastest growing category of employment across Europe.[19] Freelancers and flexible workers allow companies to be more responsive, offloading risk to their workforce and providing access to resource on tap.

CHANGE AND COMPLEXITY

Examples like the hoverboard and Pokémon Go show us that ideas, products and services spread faster around the world now. Behavioural changes like the shift to smaller orders and more flexible workforces show that leaders have started to acknowledge, even subconsciously, the potential change this represents. But how do you understand this change? Is it just about acceleration? Or is it more complicated than that?

CHAPTER 3

AMPLITUDE & FREQUENCY

What is 'change'?

It is easy to describe change in a narrow, scientific context. Imagine you are back in your school science lab with a test tube and a Bunsen burner in front of you. You put some chemicals in the tube and heat it. The liquid turns from red to blue. The change is that transformation and you can write it down in your report. You can say what chemicals you mixed and what you did to catalyse the change. You know how long it took from the moment you mixed the chemicals, or applied the heat, so you can describe the rate of change.

A+ for you. But beyond the school science lab, things get a little more complex.

Most of the changes we have considered over the last couple of chapters consist of many interlocking and overlapping events. These events are often happening in parallel. There is complexity and ambiguity about who did what and when. Though I have tried to find solid data from history books and the news coverage of more recent events, it is hard to define clear start and end points. In the real world, trying to compare the relative speed of events is enormously difficult. And given the complexity of the changes we are trying to describe, I'm not sure it adds much value.

The last chapter shows that something is clearly different about the nature of the change we are experiencing. There is a reason so many of us feel like our heads are spinning. We need language to help us describe this phenomenon and, ideally, a heuristic – a rule of thumb – to help us understand and respond to it.

I do not believe we can describe this phenomenon with a single characteristic: speed. That is just too simplistic. Even if you believe the accelerationists over the historians, does the idea that change is happening faster now help you to respond?

I believe it is more useful to think of change as having two dimensions: amplitude and frequency. This is still a heuristic, a dramatic simplification of the reality, but I think it is much more valuable in helping us to understand what has changed, and in helping us to develop a response.

WAVES OF CHANGE

Picture yourself on holiday at the seaside. You can pick your own favourite spot for this exercise.

On two consecutive days you walk down to the beach. On the first day there has been a storm out beyond the bay. It has brought giant waves crashing onto the shore. Just a few feet into the water these waves are still enormous, taller than you.

Now imagine the sound: "Crash......crash.......crash". Think about the gap between the crashes. It is long, is it not?

In scientific terms, these tall waves have great amplitude. But their frequency is low – there are long gaps between them breaking.

The next day you go back to the beach and the waves are very different. They are still strong but this time, if you waded in, they might be breaking just over your knees. Think about the sound again: "Crash...crash...crash". The gap between the waves is much shorter.

These are waves of lower amplitude, but greater frequency.

MAY YOU LIVE IN INTERESTING TIMES ...

The late 19th and 20th centuries saw sweeping, global changes that affected cultures, laws, industries, even whole economies. Advances in transport and domestic appliances transformed peoples' lives. There were drastic improvements in mortality rates, and falls in the time taken to keep a household clean and fed. And much less horse manure on the streets.

These are the types of change I described in Chapter One. Changes of great, broad consequence that took decades to be fully realized. Changes that are in many ways like the larger waves we imagined. Changes of enormous amplitude, but relatively low frequency.

By contrast, the changes described in Chapter Two are more like the second set of waves we imagined. Still strong, but much smaller and much more frequent. These are the waves we are facing today.

We are being battered by a constant stream of new ideas, products and services conducted to us at speed through our hyperconnected, highly contracted, globalized world. We are ill-equipped to deal with these high frequency changes, personally, professionally or organizationally. These are the waves that are responsible for making our heads spin.

This is not to say that the big waves have stopped. Just like at sea, we may experience multiple, overlapping waves of different sources and frequencies. The 21st century may well see changes of low frequency and great amplitude playing out over decades. Maybe we are seeing them today. The advent of the connected computer and all its fruits may well prove to be such a change. A tool of global communication, commerce and information retrieval that is small enough to fit in your pocket and cheap enough to be owned by most of the population, even in many poorer countries, is dramatic. Maybe this will be considered, in the future, on the same scale as the shift from cart to car, or the automation of a domestic chore. But from the middle of this shift, it is hard to make this judgment. We are swept up in the excitement of this change. Proud of our own age's achievements, it is hard to be objective about where our period sits in the historical context.

THE CRUX

The core idea here is a simple one. But it is the crux of this book, so I will take time to reiterate it. If we want to survive and thrive in the current age, as individuals and as leaders of groups and organizations, we must stop thinking of change in a single dimension, as a simple variable that can be either 'fast' or 'slow'.

When we talk about things as being fast or slow, we are talking about how much something changes over time. Think about the accelerator – the gas pedal – in your car. Put your foot down and one variable changes: the distance you can cover in a given period of time. An insurer might argue that other variables change as well, like your chance of bumping into the car in front. But fundamentally, when we talk about fast and slow, we are talking about change as if it is a single, simple variable like the distance travelled over time.

Change is rather more complex than that. There is not just one long arc of history along which we can plot our course and measure the speed at which we are travelling. Every person, family, town, county, country and continent has their own history. As does every employee, company and industry. Each experiences change in multiple different dimensions at the same time. Most of these changes are never of the order of magnitude to be recorded in the grand histories of our civilization. They are personal victories and tragedies, advances and falls back, periods of growth and contraction – and disruption.

I do not believe that we are in a period where we are accelerating faster along the grand arc of history. The current age will be recorded as one of great change, but only of the same order, or thereabouts, as the previous grand shifts I have discussed.

Instead, we are experiencing more, and more frequent, smaller changes. Changes that may not change our world but that can absolutely change our companies, careers, industries and sectors. In our global, hyperconnected world, small disruptive changes flow more quickly around the world than ever before.

The best way to visualize this is to think of change as a series of waves.

Waves are defined by two characteristics: amplitude and frequency. Amplitude is how far the wave moves up and down from the baseline. In other words, 'how large is a single wave?' Frequency is the speed with which the wave moves up and down. In other words, 'how many waves do we see in a given period?'

The last centuries were defined by changes of great amplitude. Giant waves crashing across society, like the advent of the washing machine or the motor car. But these waves are relatively slow to break: the frequency is low.

Today, we are in a period defined not by these great waves but by many smaller ones. Waves not of great amplitude, but of high frequency. We are being buffeted constantly by smaller waves of change, overlapping, parallel and constant. And it is this that leaves us feeling like our heads are spinning and undermines the business practices we have developed over long periods of slower change.

In our hyperconnected world, we create, iterate, adopt and abandon new ideas and products at a much greater rate than at any point in history. We can see this in adoption curves for modern products versus those such as the washing machine: our hyperconnected societies spread these ideas much more quickly now. We can see it in the turnover of the stock markets: innovators displace incumbents faster than ever before.

Waves of change are rolling over us faster than before. The important question is, why?

CHAPTER 4

ARCHIMEDES' LEVER

Afar sounds like a mythical land, conjured up for a children's story by C S Lewis or J M Barrie. But it is a real place, a low-lying region of northeast Ethiopia, rich in sites of scientific interest.

Geologists are drawn to Afar by its complex junction of tectonic plates, the giant continent-spanning slabs of the Earth's crust. Here, where it meets its Arabian counterpart, the African plate is slowly separating into distinct Nubian and Somalian plates. A few million years from now, this split will widen so far as to create a new oceanic basin.

Paleoanthropologists come to Afar to look not to the future, but to the past. A few million years into the past, in fact, to study the history of human evolution. In Afar, around the village of Hadar, are layers upon layers of sedimentary rock, rich with fossils, known as the Hadar Formation. It was here, in 1974, that researchers discovered Lucy.

Lucy is the name given to the fossilized remains of a member of the group Australopithecus afarensis – meaning 'the Southern ape from Afar' – an early ancestor of humans. Lucy and other fossils found in this area have told us a lot about how we evolved from apes. And they have shown how early we developed one of the critical characteristics that enabled our development. Something that differentiates us from just about every other creature on Earth. Something that, in many ways, is the defining human characteristic: the ability to augment our own capabilities by applying our understanding of the world.

After Lucy, many other examples of Australopithecus afarensis were found in Afar. In 2009, researchers began examining animal bones found near these fossils. What they found were scratches and marks on these bones that suggested they had been worked on. That someone, or something, had used stone tools to cut flesh and crack bones. Around 3.5 million years ago – 800,000 years earlier than previously believed – our distant ancestors were already using stone tools.

A RACE OF TOOLMAKERS

What does it mean to make a tool? And why is it important?

A tool is the solution to a problem. This means that to make a tool you need to have understood the problem. Most tools made by humans are designed to overcome our weaknesses, to amplify our capabilities, to ease our lives. Making a tool means that you have recognized your own limitations and seen that other materials around you might help you to overcome them. In this case, you have understood that hands are not sharp, or hard, but stone is. If you want to cut something, then stone is a better tool than your bare hands.

How did you come to this understanding? Maybe you fell and cut yourself on a rock. The possibility that the learning was accidental makes it no less impressive. Our early ancestors captured an understanding of the world in their minds and applied that understanding in a systematic fashion to great effect.

This application of tools to amplify our own capabilities is intrinsically connected to our evolution from this point on, not least in the development of our big brains, which came about a couple of million years after Lucy. How they came about is a question of some controversy, but either explanation requires our ancestors to have made good use of tools.

FIRE STARTERS

Big brains require lots of calories to fuel them. Your brain is responsible for consuming about 20% of the energy you expend each day. If you cannot get the calories, then you cannot have the cognitive power for language, society or all our other modern wonders.

Chimp expert Richard Wrangham, Ruth B Moore Professor of Biological Anthropology at Harvard University, believes that only fire could have fuelled the ascent from chimp to man. Fire breaks food down and makes it easy to extract calories. Compared to the chimp's diet of tough tubers and fibrous fruits, cooked foods would have been a bountiful source of calories, sufficient to support big brain growth.

The problem with this theory is that there is limited evidence that we would control fire until long after our larger brains had started to develop, leading many experts on evolution to be deeply sceptical of Wrangham's hypothesis.

What is the alternative? The primary proposition is that we focused on the richer, fleshy parts of our animal prey:

bone marrow and brains – parts only accessible with the application of tools to catch animals and crack bones. With a supply of these meaty treats, our small teeth and bellies could have extracted the calories we needed to develop our greater cognitive capabilities.

For the sake of my argument, it does not matter which hypothesis is correct. Whether the fuel for our big brains was flesh or fire, technology was at the heart of our evolutionary story.

A LEVER LONG ENOUGH

Humanity's whole history is defined by technology. Just look at how we name the ages of our development: Stone Age, Iron Age, Bronze Age, Steam Age, Digital Age. Now, perhaps, the Quantum Age. Right throughout our history, technology has been critical in determining its pattern.

In fact, technology is arguably the means by which we shape history.

"Give me a lever long enough, and a place to stand, and I will move the Earth," Archimedes is reported to have said. Throughout history, from the earliest stone tools, through the Bronze Age, Stone Age and today's Digital Age, technology has been the lever by which we move the Earth, by which we make change. If we want to understand high frequency change, then understanding how technology drives change is a very good start.

But how does technology drive change? After all, it has no agency. It is not a person with goals and desires of its own. We have not – yet – made an artificial intelligence quite that smart. The answer comes in two parts. The first is about what technology does to us, and the second is about what we do with it.

TECHNOLOGY LOWERS FRICTION

Tools, by their very nature, amplify our powers. They enable fewer people to do the work of many. They allow one person to do things they otherwise could not by reducing the effort required. The more sophisticated the tool, the more it amplifies our power.

Take language. With our voices we can reach a few people, locally. With written language we can reach hundreds of people, remotely. With the printing press? Thousands of people, nationally. Social networks? Millions of people, globally, instantly. Our power is amplified and the friction that diminishes our reach is reduced.

'Friction' in this context means any retarding force that prevents us from achieving our goal. For the voice in the example above, the friction was the dissipation of the sound waves after they left our larynx. Overcoming that friction meant sending messengers by horseback to carry information. With written language it was about how fast we could write, or with the printing press, how fast and cost-effectively we could distribute copies. Each of these modes of communication faced levels of friction that, ultimately, we overcame in order to be able to communicate an idea across the globe, instantly. We may never have had this as an explicit goal, but we always worked to take friction out of the process we were using until, finally, this incredible feat was achieved. How do we choose to use this incredible power? To share pictures of cats looking angry. But that's a different story.

Today we have lowered friction in so many areas that we can achieve a huge amount just sat on our bums on the sofa. You could start a business right there, just using your phone. In just a few hours you could complete the legal requirements, open a bank account, source a supplier, set up a website, start your marketing campaign, and sell your first product.

Don't believe me? Give it a try.

UNIVERSAL FORCE

This lowering of friction affects different industry sectors and segments of our lives at different times. But, ultimately, it touches everything, at home and at work: communication, commerce, decision-making, transport, logistics, manufacturing, design, competition.

In a low friction environment, more ideas can be created and realized. These ideas compete for attention, and new ones displace old ones at an accelerated rate. From the mid-90s onwards, with the advent of widespread, rich, digital communication, we have gone through a step change in the speed at which ideas can be translated into products and services.

As has always happened in the past, the application of one technology has accelerated the development of others. The Digital Age is one in which access to knowledge is democratized. Just about any question of fact can be answered in a matter of seconds with a few taps on a screen, or a command barked across the room to a voice assistant. Whatever we want to learn, someone has probably produced a video to teach us. Other people's solutions to our problems are released under open source licenses, building blocks for us to use in addressing any challenge.

The Digital Age has supported the rapid development of a whole range of areas, through the spread of ideas and knowledge. But it has also created a greater competitive imperative, growing the footprint of the global marketplace for products, services and ideas.

KEEPING UP WITH THE JONESES

Human beings are largely a cooperative species. You only need to open your front door to see this. Unless you are very unlucky, there will not be chaos on the streets. The fact that there is a street at all tells you a lot. We got together, formed a government and agreed a set of priorities, one of which was building roads, the cost of which we all subsidized.

For the most part we behave in a way that allows us all to exist side by side. More than that, we tend to help each other. But that does not mean we are not competitive. At home, we jealously eye our neighbour's new extension, car, or sometimes, partner. At work, the competition is even more acute. We simply cannot afford to let our rivals get ahead. If they can do more with less, or do something completely new, then it will not be long before we try to catch up or even overtake them. The alternative is bleak: failure.

Between countries, the competition is even more acute still, leading to the space race, the arms race, the Cold War and mutually assured destruction.

So, we compete. We keep a watchful eye on our peers and when they take a step forward, we aim to take two. It is not always possible. Sometimes, particularly in companies, we miss the steps our competitors have taken until it is too late. But over time, this competition drives us to make progress. And it is this competitive imperative, combined with the lowering of friction, that is driving high frequency change.

....

LIGHT SPEED

....

Human beings are not the only creatures on Earth to use tools. Seagulls will drop clams and mussels onto rocks to crack their shells. Elephants plug water holes with balls of chewed-up tree bark to prevent them from drying out. Dolphins use sea sponges to stir the sand and uncover prey. What differentiates humans is that the compounding effect of our use of tools has advanced over the years. Each new era of tools becomes the platform on which the next era is built.

We are inherently a collaborative species, evolved to live and cooperate in groups. But part of the driver for this constant cycle of development is competition. Whether it is at the state, city, company or individual level, we are always looking for that edge.

This has been the case throughout the history of humanity, but there has been a series of step changes in the speed at which we move information, products and services over the last two centuries. The replacement of the horse with the motor car, and the advent of cheap, international air freight and travel, as discussed in previous chapters, were two of them. The advent of internet communication has been the most recent and, arguably, the most dramatic.

The internet is – at least to date – the ultimate technological lubricant. By lowering the friction in communication, it has offered near-instantaneous communication between people and machines in every corner of the world. This has opened up knowledge and ideas for a wider community of people to understand them, adapt them, expand on them and commercialize them. It has created new global trade routes, introducing competition to markets from companies and freelancers operating in different time zones, cost structures, regulatory and cultural environments.

In his book *Connectography*, Parag Khanna looks at all the different ways that countries, cities, markets and communities are now interconnected, and notes that there are now more miles of connection than border. The world is shrinking. In this age of super-low friction communication, where ideas and supply chains are globally connected at light speed, the pace of both collaboration and competition are accelerated.

AMPLITUDE AND FREQUENCY

The internet may prove, when we have the benefit of hindsight, to be a change of the same order of magnitude as the shift from horse and cart to car, or the introduction of domestic automation. It certainly feels like it will prove to be so, as we live through it. Maybe we will decide it was even more important. But we cannot say yet. We do not have the perspective.

What we can say, with certainty, is that the internet is underpinning the current age of high frequency change. The internet – and ubiquitous, cheap access to it – combined with the previous iterations of world-shrinking communications and supply chain technology, has lowered the friction in our communications and operations, allowing the more rapid evolution of ideas, products and services, and their distribution to customers.

Our competitive instincts ensure that we keep driving this cycle forward, perpetuating and even accelerating high frequency change.

CHAPTER 5

THE BRAKES

"Every object persists in its state of rest or uniform motion in a straight line unless it is compelled to change that state by forces impressed upon it."

So said Newton, describing his first law of motion. What is true of objects is equally true of organizations and whole sectors: without motivation for change, things often stay the same.

Where does that motivation come from? Primarily, in our current economic system, the answer is money. People will seek to disrupt the status quo if there are profits or savings to be made in doing so. If there is no great shift in profit potential, or if the profits from a product or service are in terminal decline with little prospect of a return from any investment, then it is unlikely they will face much disruption beyond their existing challenges. Some sectors and services simply are not worth disrupting. Some lack the opportunity for disruption. There may not be – yet – any realistic technology, process improvement or other innovation that would give a new entrant a significant competitive advantage. If things cannot easily be done cheaper, faster, better, then what is the point of tackling the target sector?

Of course, to disrupt something, you need to know that it exists. Some sectors are more widely visible to potential disruptors than others. If lots of entrepreneurial characters experience a sector with clear problems, the chances are good that they will recognize the issues and believe that they can do better.

The property sector is a prime example of this. Everyone who has ever bought or rented a home has had a bad experience with a conveyancer, mortgage provider, broker, agent or landlord. 'Surely, this cannot be how it is,' we think. 'We could do better than this!'

My 6-year-old child could do better than some of the services I have experienced in this sector and so, for a while I, like many others, contemplated launching a start-up to fix them. Now, with barriers to market entry lowered by technology and globalization, more and more people are trying to disrupt the property sector. The booming 'prop-tech' industry consists of hundreds, if not thousands of companies setting out to streamline processes, strip out middlemen, automate interactions and free up data.

Speak to just about anyone in the property and con-struction sectors though, and they will tell you how slow moving and conservative they are. Some barriers will slow the pace of disruption even in the most visible and out-moded businesses. These barriers largely fall into three categories: regulation, finance and trust.

REGULATION

If an industry is heavily regulated, entry into that industry is naturally slower, more complex and, hence, more expensive that it would otherwise be. This is why large incumbents love regulation.

It may look from the outside as if big companies oppose red tape, complaining about the restrictions they find themselves wrapped in. But they are often to be found lobbying for its expansion behind the scenes. Regulation is a wonderful way to defend their entrenched position. Sometimes this defence is simply the added cost of reaching a competitive position. Think of it as the business equivalent of siting your fort at the top of a hill: if anyone wants to battle you, they must first climb up the hill.

Sometimes the defence is much more explicit, equipping incumbents with major advantages over their opponents. One example is the effective discount on business rates long offered to large telecommunications companies operating in the UK, notably the former national monopoly, BT. All telecommunications providers pay business rates on the fibre optic cables they lay in the ground. But the means by which those taxes are calculated are different for BT and Virgin, the other national carrier, than they are for new entrants, leaving the incumbents paying a much lower overall rate and the challengers at a disadvantage.[20]

Many markets need to be regulated for reasons of safety, national security or financial probity. Even without the lobbying efforts of incumbents, these will create friction that slows the entry of new ideas. But evidence shows that the level of friction created by these regulations can vary widely and a positive regulator can very much ease the path of disruptors.

Take Britain's Financial Conduct Authority as an example. The banking industry regulator created a program of 'regulatory sandboxes' to allow the testing of new ideas in a safe environment,[21] carefully overseen but with some flexibility in the application of existing rules. This has allowed new challengers to offer genuinely original alternatives to the very conservative – and very large – incumbent banking organizations, much quicker than might have otherwise been the case.

Regulation provides friction, but it is no long-term defence from disruption, and how much of a defence it provides is at the whim of the relevant regulator.

FINANCE

Arguably, the time and infrastructure required to start a disruptive business – or build a disruptive innovation – are both much less now than in the past. The services too can be much cheaper. Thanks to the internet we can now find and rapidly assemble many of the basic building blocks of business online. Company registration, bank account, payment collection: these can all be set up from a smartphone in the space of an hour with a glass of wine in your hand. We can source suppliers from anywhere in the world and access the low price that implies through marketplaces from Amazon to Alibaba. We can find freelancers to build products or help us run our businesses through networks like oDesk and Fiverr, find customers with 'weapons-grade' marketing technologies like email, social and the web. Software like Autodesk Fusion 360 allows us to design, test and produce prototypes in a single interface. Often these tools are advantageously priced for new entrants.

Even prototyping hardware has collapsed in price. When I was a small, geeky boy I soldered up a robot controller for my ZX Spectrum, steadily buying the parts with my pocket money from Tandy (the European name of RadioShack). It cost tens of pounds, maybe £50 or £60. Today I can buy something much more capable and sophisticated, off the shelf, direct from the Chinese manufacturer for a couple of pounds. And if I want to build the robot itself, I can print the parts on a 3D printer, bought for £100, and a £15 reel of plastic.

Funding is still hugely important. Building a big business, or a complex, application-ready innovation still takes time and skill and resources. This requires investment. But the barriers are much lower now than in the past.

....

TRUST

....

Perhaps the biggest barrier is trust. The social dimension.

Inside companies, this is what can halt innovation. Do people trust the new way of working not to make their lives harder or diminish their career prospects? For new entrants it is about brand: do customers trust this new entrant to deliver? This is particularly acute with finance: can you trust this unknown name with your money?

This barrier, though, has also been lowered in the modern age. We are constantly being bombarded with novel ideas, brands and products. Unfamiliarity is now our default state – how can it be anything else? Perhaps social media bubbles, to which so much social division and surprising electoral results are attributed, are so popular because they, in some way, insulate us from this constant assault of novelty.

Despite the little opportunity for evolved adaptations to deal with this shift, it is our new reality and we are having to acclimatize to it. In this environment the new is less shocking and different than it once might have been. And it is easier to trust.

FRICTION STARTS FIRES

No lack of trust will prevent a user or consumer from making a change if their current experience causes them significant pain. This is the reality for many incumbents, whether they are technologies or processes inside existing organizations, or providers to businesses or consumers outside of them. Poor customer or user experience is an incredible motivator for change. This is being demonstrated very clearly in the property and banking industries now. People are willing to take a punt on a new, even unknown, provider if their existing experience is sufficiently poor.

It is only a recent innovation that you can open a business bank account online in a matter of minutes. Only a year or two ago this would have been a six-week process. It still is with some of the legacy banks. Walk into a branch, they ask you to call instead. Call, and some banks will post out physical forms to you. In my experience, these forms do not always arrive, despite repeated chasing. Other banks will ask you to come in for an appointment where someone with very little, if any, business experience will try to understand your 21st century business and describe it in a way that fits the 20th century forms they need to fill out. And this is the best-case scenario in which you do not need any borrowing facilities and, in my case, when you have been a customer of the bank for nearly two decades.

Banks have certain responsibilities, under law and industry regulation, to maintain checks and balances.

To ensure that the people they serve are legitimate, not laundering money, and not getting themselves into difficulties. But none of these rules and regulations can excuse the incredible burden of friction that the legacy banks have incorporated into their processes. This unnecessary friction started a fire: new, innovative competitors found ways to challenge the established players. With services like Tide,[22] you can now start a business bank account, online, in minutes. And many new businesses are leaping at this opportunity.

This is not to say that there is not inertia: 'better the devil you know' is an embedded principle for many. People still need educating, their fears assuaged. But it is a good general principle that friction starts fires: anywhere an existing service, product or process causes its user pain, there is an opportunity for disruption. And the customers will likely welcome that disruption when it comes. Novelty trumps poor service every time.

CHAPTER 6

THE RISK OF HIGH FREQUENCY CHANGE

Why does it matter that the nature of change has changed? Because unless we adapt to this new reality, we and our organizations will fail.

Think back to where the book started: with the horse-sized duck and the duck-sized horses. The horse-sized duck represents the changes we are trained to deal with. It has the slow speed and large scale of change which we and our organizations are adapted to – if not perfectly. The types of change described in Chapter One: the shift from horse and cart to car, or the advent and adoption of domestic automation. Dealing with these changes is not easy. They can cause great disruption. Some people will struggle, and many organizations will fail along the way. But we at least have experience with this type of change. We know it will come and we have spent time thinking about how to deal with it, even if our execution may let us down.

Into this pattern of large-scale, long wavelength changes comes the new phenomenon, high frequency change: the duck-sized horses. These are smaller than the grand arcs of change, but large enough to disrupt single industries or businesses. They are numerous and often appear in parallel. And they move very, very fast, turning whole industries on their head in under a decade and sometimes much, much less.

High frequency change will disrupt many, if not every industry, eventually, once the barriers described in Chapter Five are overcome: opportunity, visibility, regulation, finance and trust. And it has already disrupted some, like the music industry.

OUT OF TUNE

In 2001, the music industry finally got its act together. And I was there to see it.

At the time, I was working at a marketing agency that specialized in technology. One of my clients was RealNetworks, the company that created and popularized streaming media; the technology that powers a huge proportion of our media consumption today: online radio, catch-up services, BBC iPlayer, Netflix, Spotify and more.

RealNetworks had brokered a deal with the five major music labels to build a one-stop shop for digital music that could finally challenge the threat of illegal music downloading. It was called MusicNet,[23] and I was involved in organizing the launch at a hotel in London.

The previous years had seen a dramatic rise in illegal music downloading through platforms like Napster. In February of 2001, Napster usage peaked at 26.4 million users,[24] though other networks were already on the rise. Napster itself was effectively shut down in July 2001 following lawsuits from Dr Dre and Metallica – an unlikely pairing in musical terms, but a very effective one legally. This did little to stem the flow of pirated music across the internet, however, as people just switched to alternatives like Limewire.

Meanwhile, the music industry had largely refused to engage with digital distribution. Fat on the profits from record sales of the CD, which peaked at nearly 2.5bn copies in 2000,[25] they felt no need to invest in a format they did not understand, until it became clear they had no choice.

MusicNet was a distributor of music, rather than a retailer. It would be a single platform on which brands could build their own digital music stores. Brands like the famous British music retailer HMV.

MusicNet was not HMV's first foray into digital music. It did not join the platform until 2005, having initially worked, from 2002, with Peter Gabriel's OD2 platform.[26] It sunk £10m into the launch of its new digital platform to great fanfare. Within a few years the company had tried again, switching to yet another platform.[27] But no level of success in digital was going to be enough to offset the collapse of sales on the high street. For many reasons, the company remained bound to its history of selling physical media. Ultimately, this would bring it down.

The difference in costs between physical and digital music channels was illustrated to me in 2012, not long before HMV fell into administration. I was visiting Apple's London offices, off Regent Street, for a briefing on some new product or other. The PR representative from Apple pointed me to different parts of the offices and the teams that worked in them as we grabbed a coffee from their iPad-controlled coffee machine. "Behind that wall is the iTunes team," he said, pointing. "How many people is that?" "About 17."

To be honest, I cannot remember if he said 13, 14 or 17. I was not taking notes at this point. But it was in the teens.

Apple did not break out the revenues for its iTunes store very clearly in 2012. Not by content type or by geography. But we know that line item in its accounts brought in nearly $13bn in 2012.[28] A proportion of that revenue would have been collected in Europe, where – admittedly backed by a large engineering team in the US – the team numbered in the teens.

Consider that when you look at the number of people HMV was employing. In 2012 the company made £873m,[29] down 20% from the previous year. But to do so, it employed as many as 5,000[30] people across 238 stores in the UK – more internationally. The number of stores had already shrunk by more than 50 from two years earlier.[31]

A total of £873m from 5,000 people, with all the rents, rates and logistics costs that shipping and selling little bits of plastic implies. Versus a few billion from a team in the teens, with almost no logistical costs for the digital delivery of content.

It was a stark comparison.

What made it all the more dramatic was the speed at which the transition from physical media to digital had happened: just a decade on from that deal being announced in a London hotel, digital music had largely killed off a 100-year-old industry.

TALES FROM
THE HIGH STREET

If you were at the launch of MusicNet, could you have forecast the end of high street music retail? Could you have predicted the end of Blockbuster when you first saw streaming video? Or the end of Nokia when you first tried an iPhone? Kodak after your first experience with a digital camera?

There are very few people who could have made these calls on day one. Even fewer who did. People who can see a technology and translate it into the downfall of an industry, and are willing to bet money and reputations on such disruption, are few and far between. Even those people most financially incentivized to make such predictions – venture capitalists – see their bets pay off maybe one time in 20.

In the case of HMV, Blockbuster and all the other big-brand clichés brought low by high frequency change, there was no need to be the first to recognize what was happening. They did not need to see the future on day one. Their scale gave them time in which to make the hard decisions they needed to in order to survive and even thrive in the new world. But they did not, or rather they did not make the transition until it was too late – in Nokia's case, until the CEO famously identified the company was standing on a 'burning platform'. Why?

There are multiple answers to this, which will be explored in much more detail in Part Two. But here's an outline.

First, these companies were not looking to the future, at least not in the right way. Every public company, or company of any size at all in fact, plans the year ahead as it is required.

These short-term plans are typically business as usual: last year plus or minus a few percent, depending on the prevailing conditions. Most large companies also look to the distant future, 10, 20 or 30 years hence. This is a valuable exploratory exercise, though often not given the investment it deserves. Unfortunately, it is conducted infrequently, perhaps every five years.

Medium-term planning, covering the period in which high frequency change is likely to bite, is typically very poor. It is siloed into product or service areas, or it is entirely reactive, with change programmes built around external stimuli like regulation, funding cuts or competitive challenges.

Put simply, most companies simply have no formal mechanism to spot and address novel, existential threats on the near horizon.

The second issue is one of decision-making. Power is often highly centralized in large companies, particularly power over strategic direction. And the information that decision-makers require to take appropriate action often moves very slowly through organizations and gets so polished on its journey that it loses a lot of its meaning. Decision-makers at the core of the organization are often so focused on their immediate firefights, and the threats of the competition they already know and understand, that they are insulated from the realities at the edge of the business.

The third issue is one of inertia. Changing large organizations is hard, particularly when the company has been delivering the same services for a long time and those services have returned solid profits to shareholders. The financial and contractual bounds these companies find themselves in, having developed organically and optimized over years to deliver today's service, are often incredibly hard to break. Structurally, these organizations are often super-complex and deeply integrated with organizational charts that are either indecipherable or bear little relation to day-to-day reality. Breaking these organizations down to build them up again can cause so much disruption that the process might kill the business, even if it is in service to the right end goal.

TRAINING FOR
THE NEW REALITY

Our organizations are not built for high frequency change. Our business processes do not take it into account. Our leaders are not trained and equipped to deal with it. Unless we address these issues, we are likely to see many more businesses fail.

Some might say this is the natural cycle of things. The necessary cycle of creative destruction described by economist Josef Schumpeter as being a critical part of capitalism,[32] simply accelerated. But I'm sceptical. Why does the cycle of creative destruction have to be grounded in failure? Why can we not re-engineer our organizations to be more agile? To constantly revise and reinvent themselves, operating in a permanent 'phoenix state', rising from their own ashes?

Creative destruction is a wasteful process. Remember the brakes on innovation: regulation, finance, trust? Established businesses already have the trust of their customers, or at least the best ones do. They are well-equipped to understand, even influence, legislation. And they have access to finance. Right now, these companies expend these advantages trying to fend off change, operating in the mistaken belief that they are still living in a world of multi-decade change cycles. These rearguard actions will offer ever-decreasing returns until large organizations recognize that, to survive, they need to be the agents of change, not its opponents.

This does not mean betting the future of the company on a new direction the first moment that you spot a potential disruption coming. But you do have to recognize that there are disruptive forces at work that will limit the time you have to respond. You must fight the arrogance inherent in many market-leading positions and recognize that what you deliver today may not return success tomorrow. Understanding this, you need to invest in agility today. That means improving short, long and, particularly, medium-term foresight and planning. It means accelerating decision-making based on good quality data from the edge of the organization. And it means preparing the company for change: when the time comes you need to be able to move quickly, not be bound by the past.

None of this is free, or even cheap. There is a cost to agility. But it is increasingly clear; this is the price of sustainable success.

CHAPTER 7

THEORIES OF CHANGE

High frequency change is not an idea that exists in a vacuum. It is one of several theories of the dynamic nature of change that has started to appear in the last 40 years. It makes sense to close out this section by putting the idea of high frequency change in this context.

THE AGE OF DISRUPTION

The latest phrase that has come out of the accelerationist mindset is the 'age of disruption'. Appearing splashed across opinion articles and soused over tech industry marketing materials, the idea of an age of disruption is great fodder for those looking to sell a solution. Arguably, you can put me in that camp. After all, I've sold you a book based on one idea of accelerated change.

This idea of an age of disruption, and other accelerationist mantras, has inverse effects on incumbents and new entrants. New entrants – start-ups – understand from the idea of an age of disruption that barriers have fallen. With some venture capital behind them, there is nothing to stop them displacing even the most embedded incumbent in any industry that is ripe for change. So, they charge in, emboldened.

By contrast, incumbent market players feel nothing but fear. These are the people that the accelerationists are generally selling to. The impact, and sometimes the specific intention, is that they seek out solutions that can defend them against the onrushing horde of new entrants, or faster-moving competitors.

This may seem like a cynical marketing ploy on behalf of the accelerationists, to promote this fear to sell solutions. But I think most people using this fear to sell really believe it, even feel it. After all, as I've pointed out, 80-90% of people feel like change happens faster now. And, incumbent companies really are facing new threats at an accelerated rate, albeit for the slightly more nuanced reasons I have tried to lay out. These are threats that I will go on to suggest they are ill-equipped to identify and address. It is not unreasonable to suggest that technology, or consultancy services, might be helpful in fending them off.

The problem with the idea of an age of disruption is that it lacks this nuance, or any obvious response. If we are in a general age of disruption, then surely there should be evidence that *everything* is being disrupted and that is just not true. There are many sectors that have seen little or no material change to their competitive landscape, operating structures or even core technologies, over the last three or four decades. Construction is a great example. There have been some advances in construction techniques for larger projects, and a slow shift in materials – more steel and glass, less brick. But houses built today still look fundamentally like houses a hundred years ago with only minor iterations. We have been pouring concrete in fundamentally the same way for over a hundred years.[33] Even when the adoption of technology has been enforced on the sector, as it has with the move to Building Information Modelling – a means of managing the flow of information through the construction process – it has been resisted at almost every turn.[34] I could equally point to education, transportation, government services or insurance, all of which have seen some digital reskinning but very little actual change at their core.

This lack of disruption has led to wage suppression and falling value for consumers, according to no lesser source than the IMF.[35] Every industry will have its moment at some point, but an age of disruption implies they are all happening at once.

When that disruption comes, what do you do? In an age of disruption, then surely everything is being disrupted and there is no defence. Again, I just do not believe this. There is clearly a new class of change to deal with, moving faster at a specific scale and appearing only on the near horizon before it has its effects. But this is a defined challenge to which you can respond.

The idea of an age of disruption is just too broad. But perhaps its popularity is understandable: it is simple, and from the perspective of the media industry that does so much to perpetuate it, it probably feels like an age of disruption. Media is an industry where the brakes on change have failed and the disruptive effects of technology have been most acute.

THE END OF POWER

Perhaps one of the most interesting attempts to understand the 'age of disruption' well beyond the confines of the media industry comes from Moisés Naím.

Naím has the sort of CV that makes everyone else in the room look distinctly underqualified. An international newspaper columnist and television presenter, he is also a distinguished fellow at the Carnegie Endowment for International Peace. Before this he was editor of *Foreign Policy* magazine, dean of Venezuela's leading business school, executive director of the World Bank and, oh yes, the Minister of Trade and Industry in Venezuela. Of the ten books Naím has produced, 2013's *The End of Power* is perhaps his most influential. A favourite of Facebook's Mark Zuckerberg, in this book Naím describes how power is "easier to get, harder to use and easier to lose", using examples from governments, corporations and churches.

Naím's concern is that the lack of coherent change this implies is destructive to the ends of progress. Constant disruption may be exciting and appear to imply rapid change, but this change is not always consistently for the better and, ultimately, may be anarchic.

I share some of Naím's concerns, particularly when examining the battle between corporations and start-ups. Only recently have we started to develop a more nuanced view of start-up culture. For a long time, we naturally favoured the plucky entrepreneur against the 'fat cat' capitalist behemoths they were looking to defeat, with their dodgy environmental practices, giant bonuses and poor service. What we've found instead is that, though far from perfect, the established corporations often demonstrate much better corporate behaviour than their younger rivals. Start-up culture has been exposed as often macho, misogynist and racist. Business models are often predicated on armies of low-paid, self-employed staff, and 'klepto-capitalism', making money by capturing shared assets. Aggressive approaches to tax and expectations of working to burnout are not offset by extravagant displays of philanthropy.

This is a cynical picture painted in broad brushstrokes, but there is a good amount of truth to it. The backlash has begun and there are now many more conscious, socially-aware start-ups. But it is fair to ask the question: Is constant disruption – the gale of creative destruction described by Schumpeter – the most efficient form of progress? Or would we be better off teaching large corporations to constantly reinvent themselves, maintaining their goodwill and refining their behaviour as they go?

VUCA

Perhaps the earliest example of a well thought out theory of disruptive change comes from the US military.

The early 1980s was a period of renewed tension between NATO and the USSR. If, like me, you were growing up in this period, you may have come across a comic book, and later animated film, called *When the Wind Blows*. It tells the story of a retired couple in England in the aftermath of a nuclear strike. It is terrifying and bleak. Those not wiped out in the first strike suffer a long, slow and painful death from radiation poisoning, not to say lack of food and collapsing infrastructure.

For all the fear of a nuclear attack though, these latter years of the Cold War were at least a period of certainty. Since the end of the Second World War, the US and Soviet superpowers had been at a standoff. America and its allies were committed to limiting the expansion of the communist empire. But in an age of mutually-assured destruction, with huge nuclear arsenals on each side capable of wiping out all human life, neither side was keen to escalate. And so the war remained – mostly – a cold one.

During the Cold War, there was an identifiable enemy with a clear ideology and goals. When it ended with democratic revolutions in the Soviet states in the late 1980s and early 90s, the situation became more complex. Strategic thinkers in the US military began to write about what it meant to operate in this new world and a few years later they coined the acronym VUCA to describe it: Volatile, Uncertain, Complex, Ambiguous.

VUCA crossed over from military thinking to management theory a few years later and has re-emerged periodically ever since. It seems particularly relevant in the current geopolitical climate with unexpected election results and a new cold war brewing, where the primary weapon seems to be disinformation.

High frequency change continues some of the same patterns of thinking encapsulated in VUCA. 'Volatile' means that old patterns of change no longer hold. My argument is that this is best understood in the shift from low frequency to high frequency change. 'Uncertain' means that there is less predictability in events. I would agree, albeit I do not think our predictive ability has ever been that strong. Rather, the period over which we can expect 'business as usual' to sustain has contracted and we must try to predict more frequently to stay ahead. 'Complex' means that the threats and opportunities available to us now are much more diverse. Companies face threats from all directions, as do the countries to which the military thinking was originally applied.

Whether or not the operating environment for our organizations is more 'ambiguous' now is an interesting question and probably not one for this book. You can argue the motivations are still the same as they have ever been: profit or the delivery of service to a set of stakeholders. Likewise, the threats to that ability look familiar, even if shifted through the lens of volatility, uncertainty and complexity. But the broader social environment is arguably more ambiguous than before and this, naturally, has an impact on business decisions and the characterization of those decisions in terms of 'right' and 'wrong'.

VUCA is a useful set of parameters for characterizing the nature of the disruptive forces we face, and the consideration we must make when addressing them.

TIME TO ACT

It is important to note that ideas of accelerating change are not new, nor is the type of mania represented by headlines like the 'age of disruption'. There were huge levels of excitement around the rapid rollout of railways and steam engines. The hype often got the better of people, helping to fuel bubbles that ultimately burst. But that is not to say this too was not a period of great disruption, or that a new set of behaviours was not needed to respond to the change the railways brought about.

What the three different takes on change described above show is that there is consensus, however well or ill-informed, that just like in the railway fever, something is different now. How we characterize that change and, more importantly, how we choose to respond, is the question.

Firstly, we must recognize that change is not universally accelerated across sectors, or even geographies. Every company, industry and individual is going to experience accelerated change differently, and at different times. But experience it, they almost certainly will.

The idea of high frequency change explains this. It says that while we might be in the middle of a grand, transformational change – the impact of connected computing

– we are also experiencing smaller waves of change moving at much higher speeds. These waves are many and parallel, but they are not perfectly aligned. They strike in different places in different times. The amplitude of these waves is great enough to disrupt single companies or industries. And they are visible typically on a two to five-year horizon.

Recognizing this, we must look at how we can respond. Do we have the processes in place to see these waves early, just as they start to appear? Do we have the agility to respond to their implications?

These questions, and some possible answers, are the subject of the second part of this book.

PART 2

ATHLETIC
ORGANIZATIONS

CHAPTER 8

BEYOND 'BUSINESS AS USUAL'

"Most corporations are focused on operational excellence. That means the age of creativity is over."

Ryan Shanks, director of Accenture's The Dock innovation centre

Operational excellence sounds like a noble goal. To be brilliant at doing what you do. There is nothing wrong with it, of course, if what you do is something people will continue to pay you to do into the future. If it is not, then operational excellence is just optimizing a dying service. That is probably not something you want to invest in.

Most business theory and leadership practice is, in one form or another, about optimization. About doing what you do, better, where 'better' usually means cheaper, faster or otherwise more profitably. Very little time and brain power is expended on the questions: Are we doing the right things? Will they be as valid tomorrow as they are today?

This does not matter too much if the lifespan of your business or service is measured in decades. Even if you are ultimately caught out by a major wave of change, the likelihood is that everybody else will be too. Like someone dying peacefully at a ripe old age, people will say that you had a good run.

But what if the lifespan of your business or service can now be measured in years? Months? Suddenly that endless focus on optimization does not look so wise. You need to shift the balance of your time, away from now and into next year. This is the implication of high frequency change.

This is a huge transformation to undertake, of behaviour, culture and investment. It is particularly challenging for certain classes of organization. Whether or not people will make the switch depends on their goals, their career stage and their attitude.

JAM TODAY

The first question for any leader considering this challenge is this: What do you want to achieve?

If the answer is success in the short term, then operational excellence is a reasonable target. Given shareholder pressures to deliver over fixed timescales, and the revolving door of chief executives in some places, a focus on the immediate future might be entirely justified. If your company is owned by private equity with its eyes set on short-term returns, or you are likely to be bought in the immediate future, then the chances are you will not have any choice about the horizon on which you have to focus.

The problem with this for the rest of the organization is obvious: while leadership may meet their immediate goals, everyone else may be sunk when change inevitably comes. Organizations hyper-optimized for today's proposition, pared to the bone to deliver it with maximum profitability, have very little scope for last minute transformations. There is not the bandwidth, the imagination, the skills or the capital – nor often by this point, the goodwill of customers – to support the change.

THE HOWS AND THE WHATS

Not everyone is laser-focused on the next set of results. Many leaders do have the opportunity and the desire to focus instead on stewardship. On what the organization looks like beyond their tenure. This changes the picture somewhat. In this scenario, beyond ensuring basic profitability or operation within budgets, you have the freedom to think beyond the next quarter, or year's profits, and to consider what customers might want from you in the future. You have the freedom, if not the free cash and political support, to start to range beyond today's business model.

Assuming you can get into this position, the question is, how do you do it? Even if you understand high frequency change and have the desire to insulate yourself against its more negative effects, where do you start?

The first thing to do is understand where optimization and a business-as-usual mindset undermines the prospect of accelerated change.

THE BUSINESS-AS-USUAL MINDSET

Have you ever heard of the 'cargo cults' of Melanesia?

During the Second World War, the tribes of Vanuatu and other islands witnessed forces on both sides bringing in huge amounts of supplies via air. Goods they had not seen before: canned food, manufactured clothes, Jeeps.

When the warring forces departed again after the end of the war, some of the tribespeople began trying to reconstruct the paraphernalia of air supply in a bid to restart the supply of goods. They lit signal fires, built bamboo air towers and carved headsets out of wood, listening for imaginary signals from the deities they believed would bring them riches.

The theory goes that they did not really understand how the system of air freight worked, but they thought that if they built something that looked similar, they might get the same results.

This is the way a lot of business is conducted. We operate to a half-remembered model of what a business is supposed to look like, and how a business person is supposed to behave. We assemble these archetypes in our minds from observing our colleagues and competitors, from reading books and, in a lot of cases, from fiction. We have all met people who seem to have David Brent from *The Office* as their preferred managerial archetype.

This effect is visible in all sorts of places, like the cod-formal language used by call centre staff, constantly referring to 'yourself' as if this was a more formal way of saying 'you'. You see it in presenteeism, the conscious focus of middle-management on punctuality over delivery, and the more insidious unconscious attention to just how late everyone stays. Surely if we are doing more hours, we are delivering more value? Rarely.

Most of our job descriptions bare little relation to what we do each day. Our organizational charts do not describe the organic mess of complexity that it takes to keep our mutant version of yesterday's business running. Like some extended game of Telephone (known in the UK by the possibly racist name of Chinese Whispers), practice is passed down from person to person and diverges from its intended meaning over time. Because we very rarely get the chance to look at the organization and redesign it around today's reality, we just keep doing what we did yesterday, with greater or lesser effort. And it is all based on some imaginary and half-understood operational manual from a successful time in the past that is no longer appropriate.

Even those organizations that do frequently shake up the organizational chart and review job descriptions, typically do so within the unconscious framework of the old business mode. Breaking out of it is hard.

LOOKING FORWARD

The only time we start to proactively break out of this mindset is when we believe the future will be radically different to the present. But this belief has to come from some level of foresight, and this is something that most organizations do spectacularly badly.

SHORT-TERM PLANNING

In most organizations, short-term planning is defined by the next financial period, whether that is funding or revenue-based. The very nature of this type of planning means that it is restricted to 'business as usual': you can only plan revenue and expenditure around existing streams or marginal divergences therefrom. Maybe there is a new product line planned. Perhaps a new investor, or a new channel to market. But, for the most part, the next quarter or 12 months will look a lot like the past period.

Just how true this is can be demonstrated by some figures from my work with Prophix, a Canadian software company helping to streamline and automate financial processes for mid-sized organizations. As part of my work with Prophix, we built an audit tool to allow CFOs and senior finance professionals to benchmark their progress towards becoming a 'future-ready' finance function.

One of the questions we asked was about the alignment of budget and strategy. If organizations are going to effect change in the short term, then the budget has to be mapped to the strategy. Without investment, very little is going to change. But just 12% of respondents told us that the strategy is the starting point for the budget each year. More than two thirds said there was no link between budget and strategy, or that they were aligned only at the highest level.

If the strategy does not translate into budget numbers, then the strategy – even if it is valid – will not be properly executed. The fact that there is next to no connection in the majority of organizations shows just how seriously we take foresight and planning for change in the short term. The numbers that have completed the audit are relatively small. But nonetheless it is a valuable data point about the gap between our ideal notions of what planning should look like, and the reality. We are not well equipped to steer organizations using current short-term planning techniques.

LONG-TERM PLANNING

Imagine you are in a hotel meeting room. The hotel is a good one, somewhere just outside the city. "It happens to have a good golf course attached," says the executive who called the meeting. In reality, the hotel was set up to serve the golf course, and the same could be said for the meeting you are attending.

It is an 'awayday' for the senior management team. Everyone is dressed down to varying extents. Some people look deeply uncomfortable outside of a suit and tie. There is a facilitator, all cheery smiles and waving arms. I have been that facilitator.

There are Post-it notes in all shapes and sizes and shades of neon. Giant flipcharts abound. The aim of the day is to think about the future. Maybe the horizon is five years. Maybe it is 20. You will all contribute ideas in various forms. Some will be lauded, some will be quietly ignored. Someone will be tasked with writing it all up and creating a strategy document. A document to which the organization will usually pay lip service for six months then slowly begin to ignore.

At the end of the day, everyone will retire to the bar. They will drink slightly too much, with a couple of hardier souls staying on the expensive whisky until the early hours. On Monday they will try to put the bill through expenses.

The next morning everyone will rise for a game of golf on the spectacular course that 'just happens' to be attached to the hotel, before heading home.

This, far too often, is how we do long-term planning. Maybe this is a cynical take. But if you have been in an executive role in your life, I bet you recognize some aspects of it.

This is not to say that this type of session cannot be valuable. For exploring what might be, using a framework like Scenario Planning, it can really open people's minds. It can be the place where actual strategy – one that is followed – is set. But in my experience, this is infrequently the case. Even when it is, these awaydays have two clear weaknesses: frequency and range.

FREQUENCY AND RANGE

The clue to the issue of frequency is recognizable in the title so often given to the outcomes of these sessions: the 'five-year plan'. Once set, these plans are often only revisited every few years. Sometimes well past their notional expiration date.

This may not be an issue in a world where a focus on optimization might maintain success and growth for decades. It is a huge issue in a world of high frequency change, where multiple, materially disruptive issues may have appeared on the near horizon within the lifecycle of the plan and had their impact before anyone has sat down to consider them.

The problem of range – or rather lack of it – comes from who is in the room when the planning session begins. Beyond the facilitator, all too often it is only the executives, and some board members. This group tends to be very insulated from, or resistant to, ideas that might challenge the status quo.

In my experience it takes only a matter of months of exposure to a working environment to begin to absorb its prejudices. It is why I limit my consulting engagements to a maximum of six months. If I spend any longer than that with a client, I've found that I start accepting sentiments that would have scared me on the first day. I stop challenging phrases like "this industry is different," and "that will not work here."

As a consultant, it is my responsibility to challenge these ideas because they are so infrequently true. These are the sentiments that doomed so many big names to fail to see what was coming for their business, a combination of ignorance, arrogance and subconscious self-reassurance to which we can all fall prey. It is hard to keep challenging the status quo and ultimately almost all of us stop doing it, or at least turn the volume down, for the sake of an easy life.

Even strong-minded non-execs with expertise from elsewhere – the people who are brought into boards to challenge the existing thinking – have typically been engaged with the organization for years. The addition of one or two new non-executives every few years does little to disrupt the groupthink and except for the most strong-willed and outspoken – often the first to be replaced – the whole group returns to a very settled mode of thinking.

Any attempt to build a planning process that embeds adaptability needs to address both issues: frequency and range.

CHAPTER 9

MAKE IT SO

The inability to plan for anything but business as usual is only one of the weaknesses afflicting organizations facing high frequency change. Once you have a vision of the future, you then need to build a response and execute it and do so in a time frame that will make that response meaningful.

This lack of rapid decision-making ability and slow business transformation is not a new problem. Many people know the story of the lengths that IBM went to in order to enter the personal computer market rapidly, back in the early 1980s. Faced with the fast-rising popularity of devices like the Apple II, the device on which Apple's initial success was built, IBM's leaders recognized the potential of the personal computer and decided they wanted a piece of the action. Designing this new device inside the strictures of an organization set up to build and maintain large-scale corporate computing would have been near impossible. The design standards and behaviours were just incompatible with speed and agility.

Instead, IBM created an engineering team outside of the normal strictures of the giant corporation – the 'Dirty Dozen'. This team prototyped rapidly, using off-the-shelf parts rather than designing its own. This approach allowed IBM to enter the market quickly, though it ultimately handed the greatest success to Intel and Microsoft, which provided the central processing unit (CPU) and software respectively, and which went on to sell the same components to all of IBM's competitors, allowing them to build 'IBM compatible' PCs.

Some might see this strategic choice as a failure on IBM's part, not to own the PC market in the long term. But there is a solid argument that this was a great success: IBM helped to create a standardized PC market which might never have achieved the same scale without such openness. More PCs meant more server and software sales, feeding back into IBM's long-term success.

INNOVATION VS TRANSFORMATION

'Skunkworks' has become a generic term for such product innovation teams, flying under the radar and outside the normal corporate limitations. The name comes from Lockheed's rapid development team back in the Second World War that worked on the P-80 Shooting Star, the US Air Force's first jet fighter. This team has become the prototype, in name and function, for many such operations. They exist because organizations and their leaders have long understood that the processes for optimizing business as usual can limit the development of tomorrow's model.

With the right protections around them, these start-ups within the business can be enormously successful. But they have their limitations. The two examples above – and there are many more – are all about new product development. They are small teams that can be isolated or at least freed. Yes, they may have ultimately changed the business, perhaps most famously with the development of Apple's Macintosh machine, but they were not representative of the entire business model. How can you possibly change that in a short period of time?

This is clearly an enormous question, one of culture and people as much as finance and process. But there are two critical issues that stand out for me: firstly, how and when do you take the decision to make this large-scale change? And secondly, how do you prepare an organization for this scale of change?

THE BIG DECISIONS

Consider the story of HMV from earlier in the book. This was an organization that was seeing its fundamental business model – selling physical media – undermined. The leadership knew this. It was acknowledged in the group's annual reports. At what point should they have been expected to respond to this trend and move wholesale into digital, or make another fundamental shift to save the business?

Was it when the first legal music downloading service was launched? Five years later the company was still growing revenue at double-digit rates, eliminating debt and paying dividends. Any truly radical shift at this earlier point would undoubtedly have been rejected by shareholders and seen a change in the executive team.

Maybe it should have made more radical changes three years later after a difficult year that saw the decline of sales of physical music and video? But just these three short years later, the group was already having to refinance, and was closing stores. Even rapidly growing digital revenues could not offset the incredibly rapid decline in CD sales.

What is clear from this example is that the decision point is incredibly tricky to judge for radical action. And that most traditional companies are tightly bound to their existing operating model, both culturally and financially – in HMV's case with its store leases.

You cannot discuss the process for making better strategic decisions without considering the structure of the organization within which those decisions are made.

SILOS AND MONOLITHS

I frequently hear from leaders in organizations that they are trying to 'break down silos'. But what they mean by a 'silo' varies.

In some instances, what they mean is that different functions in their organization are highly territorial and poor at communication and collaboration. Finance, for example, can cause huge problems if it is not a collaborative function, leading to rancorous budget-setting exercises and poor information flow through the rest of the organization. Likewise, a marketing function operating in isolation can be extremely detrimental to the business.

In other situations, silos are parallel vertically-integrated lines of business that have grown up organically. Each product or service-based fiefdom has evolved its own customer interface, systems, processes, behaviours and even language. Sometimes, whether through mergers and acquisitions or just poor integration, they have even evolved their own finance and billing systems. Each silo has little interaction with its peers.

Neither of these situations is attractive from an optimization perspective. There is much duplication of effort, unnecessary administration and lots of friction in day-to-day operations. So, leaders naturally want to break these silos down and build a more integrated operation where there is close cooperation between functions and no overlapping capabilities between lines of business.

This leaves us with three possibly different versions of the same business:

A. Suffers from silo mentality in business functions resulting in internal friction.
B. Suffers from vertical silos around lines of business, resulting in duplication of effort.
C. No silos. Tightly integrated functions supporting lines of business with no overlap.

It is clear which of these is best from an operational excellence standpoint. But which of these would you like to be running if you had to make radical change?

A is going to be a political nightmare, and the lack of cooperation between functions might doom you before you start. So, it is between B and C, and out of these two, I would choose B.

Imagine as part of your change process, you are going to shed some lines of business and introduce new ones. In B, you can largely pare off the failing lines with little implication for the rest of the business. It might be bad for the people in those lines of business, but the others will be largely unaffected. The separation will be relatively clean, whereas with C, you have to unpick close integrations in systems and processes. Here, you might have developed deep inter-reliance between lines of business as part of the optimization process. Change is far from impossible, but it is much more challenging, politically and functionally.

No organization looks exactly like A, B or C. They are usually some combination of all of them. They might have an efficient shared service function for some capabilities, but others that refuse to integrate. They might have some lines of business that work closely together and others that are totally isolated. I've worked, across the public and private sector, with organizations that have just about all of these possible patterns. But they have all shared one characteristic: when the time came to change, they found it incredibly difficult.

NEOPHOBES OR NEOPHILES?

We assume change will be hard in a corporate context, in large part because of the people. This is why we have so much research and practice devoted to change management. If you are putting people's livelihoods at risk and asking them to change what they do for 8+ hours each day, then there is bound to be concern and pushback. We are naturally neophobic.

This is not the standard human condition; it is a function of the workplace. As the physicist and neuroscience writer Leonard Mlodinow pointed out in a lecture at the RSA, human beings are neophiles by nature. We love the new, the innovative, the original. It is part of what drives us forward as a species. The reason we reject change so strongly in a corporate context is because it is so often negative; part of a plan for restructuring that might cost us our jobs or slow our career progression.

Restructuring, then, has become a word that means job losses and fear. But what if the heart of the problem, and the challenge of change, comes not from the people but the need to restructure at all? All three of the models laid out above are very poor starting points for change. The one that is the least poor from a change perspective is one that most organizations have spent years trying to move away from, in a bid to be more efficient. This is not to say that they are wrong to do so, but rather to question our whole approach to change management.

Should we be focusing all our efforts on optimizing our businesses when it is increasingly clear that change will come with greater frequency? Should we just accept the enormous challenge that the people aspects of change management will present when the time comes to change our highly optimized organizations? Or should we perhaps be thinking about changing the way our organizations are structured today to minimize the friction in future changes, even if that costs us some portion of our efficiency?

FORESIGHT FAILURES

This might sound like an admission of defeat from a futurist but, as I will explain in future chapters, no foresight methodology is foolproof. Forecasting is incredibly difficult, and to do so with enough confidence to make radical changes to a profitable, successful business is nearly impossible, especially when that business has a large number of stakeholders.

We need good foresight tools to have any hope of steering our organizations through the increasingly volatile and complex environment of high frequency change ahead of us. But they can only ever be part of the answer. We need to look at how we will respond when we see the future, and when that future resolves with sufficient clarity for us to be able to make the case for change. By this time, we may need to move incredibly quickly, and that means changing the way we make decisions and preparing our organizations for very rapid change.

CHAPTER 10

THE TRAITS OF AN ATHLETE

Principals of sustainable success in an age of high frequency change.

The athlete, television presenter and owner of the biggest laugh in show business, Kriss Akabusi, tells a great story of how he and the rest of the British 4x400m relay runners beat the Americans in the 1991 World Athletics Championships. It is not about spirit or heart, fitness or training. It is about strategy.

Like many of the greatest athletes, Kriss and the other members of the team, read the game. They knew that to beat the physically superior US runners, they had to do something different. So, they switched the order of their runners to do something deeply unconventional in relay: they put their fastest runner, Roger Black, into the first leg. Traditionally, he would have run the last, 'anchor' leg.

This switch surprised the Americans, but also gave the British a psychological advantage. Rather than entering the second leg behind, and trailing for the rest of the race, they entered it marginally ahead. They went on to win the race with the American runners still clearly in shock, receiving their medals from an unfamiliar step on the podium.

The strategic vision that enabled this victory is just one of the traits of great athletes that organizations need to replicate in order to be future-ready.

PERCEPTION

Perception is about the acuity of the senses. Athletes have an enhanced ability to see, hear and sense the environment around them, and they know the position and state of their own bodies. Whether it is innate or from extensive training, or a combination of the two, athletes outperform the rest of us in their ability to understand what is happening when things are moving quickly.

In an organizational context, this translates into ultra-sharp senses for what is going on in the market: with customers, partners, suppliers and other influencers of success. Athletic organizations hone these senses until they are highly acute, keeping a watchful eye out for signals of changing fortune. How? They have smooth, slick data flows into and through the structure of the business, routing relevant information to the right people, fast. Or they allow people at the edge of the organization to respond to the information they see. Both of these possibilities are explored in subsequent chapters.

For great athletes, like Kriss Akabusi and the relay team, this near-field sense of what is happening translates into a sense of where the game is going. The greatest footballers – soccer players, for those on the other side of the pond – are renowned for their vision and foresight, as much as their on-the-ball skill. The legendary midfield playmakers can read the game and make plays before anyone else sees them, knowing that their winger will be on the end of a 40-yard, cross-field pass before they strike the ball.

Athletic organizations too need great foresight; the ability to read the game and translate that understanding into action, to recognize threats and opportunities early. Foresight, or horizon-scanning, processes in most organizations are infrequent and informal – part of a wider weakness in planning. They are activities for the occasional corporate awayday, not an accepted component of day-to-day management and operations. This has to change. Not only do leaders need to embed in their cycle much more frequent and formal attempts to look beyond the organization's walls, but members across the organization need to be encouraged to watch, consider and share learning from other facets of their lives and adjacent or relevant markets and environments.

REACTION

Great athletes have fast reactions; they do not just read the environment and the game, they respond fast to the input from their senses. This is a decision-making capability that translates directly into decision-making capability in organizations.

This is about the deeply interconnected processes of foresight, planning and communication. Future-ready organizations understand the impact of external changes on their key audiences– staff, shareholders, customers and partners. They use foresight to see these changes first but are also set up for rapid reactive change when necessary.

The processes to build and communicate a response quickly, in a format that compels action, are well rehearsed.

AGILITY

Of course, the greatest perception and reactions are worth nothing in an athlete without the physical agility to translate plans into real action. Organizations, like athletes, need to be fit.

A fit and future-ready organization has well-defined muscle groups, just like an athlete. It is clear which parts of the organization perform which functions. Their inputs and outputs can be clearly understood and measured.

Flexibility has been engineered out of most organizations. They have been built, or more often allowed to evolve, to do what they do, and not for the possibility they need to change what they do, frequently. Though few organizations approach real efficiency, it is this notional goal that has defined their shape.

Today, agility is more important. Organizations need to be designed explicitly for regular realignment to new markets, products, services and objectives. Structured in functional blocks that can be more easily broken down and reassembled, with clear data flowing across units and out to management.

TRAINING THE GREATS

Athletes, whether they are a hurdler, footballer, gymnast, racing driver or a fighter pilot, are people who operate in fast-moving environments. Three characteristics make them particularly fit for these situations:

- Strong senses, to take in what is going on around them.
- Fast responses: a nervous system that will carry the messages from the senses to their brain, and a brain that can rapidly determine how to react.
- A fit body, allowing them to act rapidly on the instructions that come from the brain.

Organizations are no different. In a high frequency change environment, organizations need to have good senses for what is changing, even foreseeing what is about to happen. They need to be able to develop a response to those stimuli rapidly. And they need to be able to act, fast.

Like great athletes, future-ready organizations rarely develop on their own. They are surrounded by a team of trainers and professionals who help to keep them on course, developing every part of their capabilities to maintain a high-functioning whole.

The Applied Futurism that I practise is an attempt to equip organizations with these characteristics, and this book forms part of that mission. Futurists are not the athletes of the organization; they are the coaches, building a training regimen for fit and future-ready organizations. The goal is to transform client organizations into athletic specimens who can build and sustain success over the long term. In my work I try to inspire, and sometimes shock, leaders into investing more time and money into foresight. I help them to build streamlined planning and communications practices, so that they can assemble a response quickly and share it with those affected. And I put this in a framework for organizational design that ensures the ability to react with great speed and flexibility. These processes and frameworks are laid out over the next few chapters.

CHAPTER 11

SHARPER SENSES

Why operational response
is so important in an age of
high frequency change.

Waterstones was failing when James Daunt took over. He changed a lot, but one of the most significant things he gave to these stores was more autonomy. His background in running an independent book store had taught him that you must know your customers and what they will buy. If you are responsible for choosing the books you will sell, you will do a better job of selling them. So, Daunt ended the centralized buying of books and allowed each branch of Waterstones to select its own range.

The result was dramatic: returns of unsold books fell from 20-25% to just 4%.[36]

What Daunt had done was put decision-making closer to the customer and pushed responsibility away from the centre of the organization. These are two critical characteristics for any organization that wants to be more responsive.

EXPECTATIONS ARE PORTABLE

One of my first major clients when I started work as a futurist was a large London borough, Enfield. The local authority was, like its peers, undergoing huge transformation. In the post-crash climate of austerity, it was losing about half its budget and, as a result, half its staff, in just a few short years. One of the big four consultancy groups had been brought in to handle the transformation, alongside existing staff and an army of contractors. The aim was to condense the organization down into a form that would fit the tight new budgetary constraints.

Through various connections I got a call one day and was asked to come and have a chat with the chief executive. His challenge was this: he was confident that the transformation programme would leave him with an authority that would be viable, but it would not be anything like what you would design if you were to start from scratch. He wanted an ideal against which to compare, and so I was tasked with designing a local authority fit for the 21st century and, along the way, engaging with the existing transformation programme to help with pointers based on my digital experience.

This was a fascinating brief and the outputs of it formed the beginning of the model I will describe for agile organizations in Chapter 14. But one of the first things I learned was about the portability of expectations.

Enfield's digital service, like most councils in 2013, was not very strong. It was desperately short of people with digital skills beyond basic website maintenance. While there was clear ambition, the gap between this and reality was large. As part of the learning and development process, the council engaged with local citizens to gather feedback. What they quickly learned was that people's expectations for council digital services were very high but not in terms of functionality: most people engage with the council infrequently and for relatively mundane tasks. They have no desire for the council to expand its services into new areas. Rather the expectations were for performance, speed and ease. These were set not by people's previous engagements with government services – they may have had none in any case. They were set by engagement with Amazon, Facebook, eBay and the other digital giants.

Even though these organizations were running completely incomparable services, they defined people's expectations for any digital interaction. As Simon Eckstein, now Head of Strategy and Design for Digital, Data and Technology at the Department for International Trade, but then a business analyst responsible for running some of the feedback sessions at Enfield, notes: "It was helpful in trying to push a bold agenda. But it was also a stick to be beaten with."

This 'portability of expectation' has since been confirmed by a number of studies. Notably, KPMG Nunwood's annual customer experience study shows that new entrants to a market, companies without the burden of legacy technologies, consistently set the pace and drive the continuing increase in customer expectations. Incumbent organizations are always playing catch-up.

HARDER, BETTER, FASTER

Service, as you might expect, is an incredibly important factor in customer loyalty. I worked with Salesforce Commerce Cloud (formerly known as Demandware) on a project on the future of retail in 2016 and, as part of that project, we surveyed about 7,000 16-35-year-olds around the world – 'millennials'. This group was incredibly clear about what retailers could do to create loyalty. After price, service was their number one priority. Speed of delivery was rated by 60% as a key factor in securing their loyalty. Nearly half focused on slick and easy payment options.

Overall, the picture we saw was of a customer base that prized a low friction shopping experience over almost everything else. They wanted to be able to get the things they wanted, when they wanted them, with maximum speed and minimum fuss.

This focus on high speed, low friction interactions follows a general pattern of rising expectations driven by advances in communications technology. When written communication was the only option, the Pony Express, offering transcontinental communication in the US in just ten days, seemed incredible. But just 18 months after it launched, it was superseded by the transcontinental telegraph. The new benchmark was set and everything else would then be compared to it.

Now we have instant access to everything at our fingertips, including many products and services that were, in the past, only available with a physical interface: books, news, music, films, games. Even those things that remain bound to the physical world can be delivered in just a couple of hours if you live within range of an Amazon depot and need something in its stocked range. It should be no surprise that our expectations have risen accordingly.

So, what can organizations do to respond?

The answer comes back to the Waterstones story: recognize that those at the edge of the organization are closest to the customer and often have the best intelligence.

EASTER EGGS

At the 2015 Social Media Communications Awards, the Grand Prix – the top award – was given to LIDL and social media marketing agency Cubaka. Judges were impressed with the incredible speed at which LIDL had turned social media intelligence into merchandising decisions.

The story goes like this: on 25 March 2015, Zayn Malik left One Direction, devastating teenage fans around the world. This was poor timing for LIDL, which had just rolled out a range of One Direction Easter eggs onto shelves and was making something of a splash about them. If you are not familiar with LIDL, it is a German discount grocer that was still just entering the consciousness of many UK shoppers in 2015. Though the company had been present in the UK since 1994, it was only latterly that it had been seen as a serious alternative to the major supermarket brands for more middle-class shoppers. It certainly was not known for carrying big brands.

The news broke at LIDL via its social media marketing agency, Cubaka. Here the person responsible for monitoring social channels fed the news about Zayn back to a merchandising executive at LIDL, who took the decision to respond positively to the news with a 20% discount. After all, one fifth of the band had left, so why not knock one fifth of the price off?

This was conveyed back to the social media agency who wrote a tweet in the perfect tone to appeal to the broken hearts of One Direction fans across the country. The news spread fast with the tweet going viral, attracting fans into LIDL stores and doing its brand no harm at all in the eyes of the influential fans.

What so impressed the judges of the award, of which I was one, was that the whole process, from social media intelligence to major merchandising decision, took just 20 minutes.

I bumped into a board member for one of the larger supermarkets a couple of years later and asked them whether they could replicate this feat. Even two years later, she said it would be impossible. Such a decision would have had to go through layers of management approval. In her estimate, it would have taken days rather than minutes to develop such a response.

LISTEN AND ACT

LIDL and Waterstones succeeded because people close to the market had the power to take action on the information they saw. Pushing power to people at the edge of the organization, who are naturally closer to the realities of the market, is arguably the optimum solution to improving operational responsibility. It requires training and structure to ensure that people feel empowered to take decisions and know that they can make mistakes safely, within a defined set of parameters. It requires some oversight, so that if people do over-reach their powers, it is clear to them and to the organization.

All this takes time, thought and investment. But it costs a fraction of the alternative approach, which is accelerating the flow of information through the organization to those people already empowered to take decisions.

This usually starts with a large investment in technology: business intelligence or analytical systems. Underpinning this is some grand project to unify and order the organization's data into one single 'data lake' or 'information warehouse'. Projects like this can deliver value, and every leader should be empowered with good analytical tools for their organization. But these are primarily strategic tools, not ones to drive a rapid tactical response, and the two objectives are often confused. In part, this comes from an unwillingness to release control but also from a natural human desire for order. Information in organizations is always messy. The desire to order it is natural, and the belief that value can be extracted from that order is the way we justify the investment to ourselves. But ordering a large organization's data is the work of a lifetime. Waiting until it is done to extract value from the data is a sure way to kill a business.

Pushing power to the edge of the organization does more than accelerate the response time. It gives the recipients of the power greater purpose and responsibility. It creates a more engaging job for them and, done right, makes them feel part of the organization's success. It also reduces the flow of unnecessary communications through the organization, stripping away more noise that might obfuscate the really important signals. And it reduces the massive over-centralization of control that has been a characteristic of many of our large organizations – public and private – for too long now. This decentralization is a critical characteristic of future-ready organizations that I will discuss in Chapter 14.

LET SALESPEOPLE SELL

I'll finish this chapter with a last case study. I was working with a very large engineering company, one that makes parts for large manufacturing plants around the world. During a workshop, we started to discuss the idea of decentralizing power and one woman raised a recent issue they had uncovered and addressed. She had been tasked with streamlining the approval process for sales credit. On examining the situation, she realized that the threshold for getting approval for credit was set at a fraction of the average order value. She guessed that at some point in the past, a customer had been extended a line of credit that they had never been able to support, and so to avoid this someone in finance had placed a very conservative limit on the amount of credit a salesperson could offer without authority. This authority had to be secured on every order, creating an enormous amount of administrative traffic in the business and slowing the company's response time to customers.

The answer was simple: raise the threshold. Sure, she could improve the process, but this would have a fraction of the effect of just cutting the number of approvals that needed to be given. In the event, she was given approval to raise the threshold albeit to still well below the average order value. Nonetheless, the effect was dramatic. Suddenly salespeople could respond much faster to a large proportion of orders, improving service and speeding sales. Less of their time was wasted on administration and could be focused on customer relationships. Administrators' time in finance and elsewhere was freed to focus on the future, not the past, including other process improvements.

This sounds like the sort of case that should be too simple to be real inside a multinational, multi-billion-dollar company. And yet it is incredibly common. Stories like this abound. I heard a similar story just a few days later about warehouse staff needing four different signatures to approve leave – signatures that went four or five levels up the organization. We have a general culture of hyper-centralization of power in our organizations, and a real conservatism about giving control and responsibility to those who perhaps have the best prospect of using it valuably to serve our customers.

In order to build future-ready, athletic organizations, we must address this culture and change it.

CHAPTER 12

STRATEGIC SENSES: BEYOND THE BLINKERS

What is the next big thing? The one that will make your company's next fortune? Or take your organization out at the knees? Where will it come from? How far away is it?

In an age of high frequency change, the answer to that last question is probably 'closer than you think'. As I've shown, ideas, products and services spread faster around the world now. Their development cycle is shortened in many cases too: people are building based on an established web of widely accessible knowledge and off-the-shelf components, whether they are building government services, medical treatments or consumer products. There are brakes on that innovation – finance, regulation, cultural acceptance – but, fundamentally, we have to be able to plan now for major changes happening in our sectors on a shorter timetable.

This is something that organizations on the whole are very bad at. As I have suggested in earlier chapters, most short-term planning is poorly executed and based almost entirely on some version of business as usual. Long-term planning can be good, but it is insufficient to identify challenges on the near horizon since most techniques are explicitly focused on the third horizon – the distant future of 20 years hence.

So, what is the answer?

Athletic organizations need a new technique for scanning the near horizon. One that can be repeated frequently, which means that it cannot be too time or resource intensive. It does not have to be complete: the process will be re-run in a few months, so anything missed or dismissed the first time will likely be captured when the picture becomes clearer, or the threat or opportunity more real.

The technique I use for this is very simple. I call it 'Inter-sections' because it is designed to identify the intersections between the macro trends transforming our organizations and lives, and the existing pressure points where these trends are likely to have the greatest effect.

PRESSURE POINTS

What frustrates you at work each day? What stops you being as productive as you can be? Ask your colleagues these questions and you are likely to get a torrent of responses. It is a cathartic exercise, and an enormously valuable one. These are the first questions to ask when trying to understand how the major technology-driven trends will affect your organization.

Ask a cross section of your colleagues and collate the answers, and you will have a list of weak points in your organization. These weak points are where incoming trends are likely to apply stress. They are where competitors can start to challenge you. They are reasons for customers to abandon you. They are the issues that might cost you great staff, or great partners.

Expand the questions beyond individuals and ask people what they think stops their team or department from being as good as it can be? The biggest issues they face at that scale? Then ask them about the organization as a whole. What are its biggest weaknesses? If you are feeling really brave, ask them about other functions in the business, but keep it confidential if you do.

Compare these answers about the business with what your sector media and analysts say. Some issues will not be unique to you: everyone in your sector will be facing them. The responses from your people will largely be 'internal pressure points', ones that may be common to your peer organizations but are not structural. Common examples are failures in technology, process or internal communications. Sometimes all three. For example, I found the critical issue at the heart of one consulting client's company when a junior administrator told me that they had a 'chasing culture'. "Nothing gets done unless I pick up the phone," she said. Instantly it was clear that any investment the company had made in processes and the technology to support them had failed.

Sometimes internal pressures are about infrastructure. One client's cost base was heavily tied to its long lease on warehouse space and its fleet of vehicles. However, the size of vehicles they needed was changing and new software systems looked set to slash the required warehouse footprint. This was a huge pressure point. It wasn't necessarily unique to them but it wasn't an issue the whole industry shared.

These shared issues, discussed by the media and the analysts will be 'external pressure points', structural issues that everyone is facing and that might require a sector-wide solution or an original response. For example, interest rates or trade tariffs might affect everyone in the same industry. In the public sector it might be austerity budgets or the ageing population. Maybe particular supply lines are being challenged by declining availability or raw materials, or climate change.

Collate your research and write two lists: internal and external pressure points. This may sound like a long job but with a little practice it can be conducted pretty quickly. A templated survey email to a random cross section of the organization sent out every six months should give you 20-30 responses to work through at most. Do not try to survey the whole organization at once as you will never get through all the data and the exercise will stall. If you do not have internal tools for this there are loads of low-cost options like SurveyMonkey that will allow you to quickly build a template and collect answers.

Scanning the sector media for key issues is a learned skill. Get subscriptions to two or three sector magazines or websites if you do not have them already. Or just scan their weekly email bulletins. Jot down the issues that crop up again and again, and you will have a pretty good idea of the external pressure points before you start. This can guide you in seeking out analyst reports that can provide you with more depth on these issues if needed. These can be expensive, typically thousands of pounds each unless you subscribe to a particular analyst house's output, so it is worth selecting carefully.

By the time you have run the exercise a few times, the whole information gathering process around pressure points should not take more than a couple of hours.

MACRO TRENDS

Technology is the greatest driver of change right now. Traditionally, business thinkers considered the range of change drivers under the rough groupings of political, economic, social, technological, legal, and environmental factors. Of these, technology is the only one that is both consistently moving at an exponential pace and whose effects are persistent. While economies see-saw and laws can be changed, there is no 'uninventing' technology. This is why clients tell me consistently that technology is at the top of their list of strategic issues. Even just days after the Brexit vote, one German Global 500 company I was working with told me that technology remained at the top of their list, a much bigger concern than possible tariffs or trade challenges. Even the risks presented by climate change are currently displaced from the top of the to-do list by technological change and threats. This may not be the right focus for the sake of humanity but is, nonetheless, the most common.

This is why, when looking towards the near horizon, I focus on technology-driven changes. It is not that the others are not important, but they should be largely captured in your external pressure points. Technology might not always be the biggest driver of change: in a couple of decades, the environment may have claimed its proper place and action on its defence may be perceived as more urgent. Note that this may already be the case in some geographies and for some organizations: everyone's future is unique, and so are the priorities that will shape it. This is an important note about futurism: you are rarely trying to foresee 'THE future'; it is all about 'YOUR future'.

There are five key trends that I focus on, all underpinned by the lubricating effects of technology:

- Change
- Choice
- Power
- Speed
- Shape

CHANGE

The first effect is the subject of this book: high frequency change. High frequency change does not necessarily play into your Intersections; it is more the reason for running the exercise at all. But it is worth reminding people, if you are running the process as a group, why it is important and what drives this sense of urgency.

CHOICE

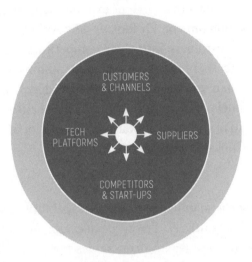

THE CHOICE COMPASS

Technology lowers the barriers to entry into just about every market. This means that your challenges are not likely to come from traditional sources. When considering threats and opportunities on the near horizon you must look in all directions. To help people think about this I use a simple model called the 'Choice Compass', though you could equally call it the 'Competition Compass' as threats are coming from all around: your customers may be looking to do things for themselves; your partners may be building competitive products; major tech platforms may be entering your market space or enabling others to do so. The worst-case scenario is often when these different players come together: witness the access to international markets that major tech platforms have given to Chinese manufacturers, bypassing retailers to an extent exponentially greater than in the first dotcom era. Or look at how Airbnb has turned the hotels' customers into their competitors. On a more positive note, there may be many more options in the supply chain than you have previously considered, and many more channels of communication with the customer. You can map all of these collaborations and potential competitors on a Choice Compass.

POWER

Technology is augmenting human capability, both physically and cognitively. Fewer people can now do more, resulting in some leading companies having productivity levels that are incredible by historical standards: companies like Apple and Visa make more than $1m in revenue per employee. Exoskeletons to augment human strength and protect workers from injury in warehouses and on building sites are now available for just a few thousand dollars. Robot bricklayers can enable one person to do the work of three. And this is before we get into the impact of machine learning and artificial intelligence. Even relatively simple workplace automations are starting to diminish the need for junior members of staff in many fields: law, accounting, customer service and more. This is a critical consideration for any organization struggling with margins, efficiency or productivity: it is almost certain someone else will do it, not just cheaper, but better, soon.

SPEED

As noted in the previous chapter, customer expectations for service are rising. But this is just part of a wider trend of rising expectations for the speed at which organizations absorb information and respond to it. The 24-hour news media, social networks and widespread access to share trading, have all played their part. Operationally and strategically, organizations need to be able to process what is happening and respond with alacrity. Those that do not will be punished by public sentiment, or the markets.

SHAPE

Low friction communications have allowed us to change the shape of organizations. First, there was a growing interest in outsourcing: if the friction between two businesses is low, even if one is geographically remote, then why not put services where they can be run most cheaply? Then came the fashion for remote and home working: if our employees are always on, why do we need to put them at a desk? Most recently we have seen a growing use of freelancers, an army of which can be sourced and engaged through digital channels like oDesk and Fiverr, as and when required. The latest iteration of this trend is more about technology than people: why build all the components you need to run a business when other people can run them for you? You can assemble an operational business from a stack of digital building blocks pulled from a range of sources. More on this in Chapter 14.

A FRESH PAIR OF EYES

When you are preparing your Intersections session, it is critical to do some reading around these areas or bring in someone with external expertise. Clip articles, watch videos, dig into news sources you would not ordinarily access. See what people are doing in adjacent industries, or other countries. Open your mind to how these trends could affect you.

This is why I called this chapter 'Beyond the blinkers'. In my experience, it takes very little time spent in an organization before the blinkers come down and you are blinded to what is going on elsewhere in the world. When challenged with new ideas and possibilities, people with the blinkers on tend to give answers like "that won't work here" or "this company is different". These sentiments are almost never true. Sooner or later these macro trends affect every organization in every sector that I have worked in, from charities to global corporations, universities and governments.

If you do not feel equipped to take off your own blinkers, find someone to help you. Get someone in with a fresh pair of eyes. Someone from a different sector. Someone from a marketing agency or management consultancy. Maybe your accountants or even lawyers. If you can find one, hire a futurist. Do not use the same people each time: it is diversity of perspective that counts and that is as true of the people in the room. Intersections is best run as a small group exercise where people with different perspectives can contribute. Get people of different ages, seniorities, roles, sexes, races and cultures around the table and, again, do not always use the same people.

SOURCE, STRIKE, SUBSTANCE

There are many ways to map the Macro Trends against the Pressure Points you identified but the simplest way I have found is this:

- **Source**: Pick one of the possible competitors from the Choice Compass.
- **Strike**: Pick one of the Pressure Points that seem most challenging.
- **Substance**: Consider what a challenge might look like based on one of the Macro Trends, coming from the competitor you have selected and landing at the Pressure Point you identified.

This will get you thinking about risks you have not considered but also opportunities. Consider the Source is not a competitor but a potential supplier or partner. How could they help you to ameliorate the Pressure Point you are facing?

This approach often becomes a way to present issues and opportunities that have become apparent, rather than a way to discover them. Once you have run the process a couple of times, it becomes second nature to start connecting the dots between your Pressure Points and the Macro Trends. The only question then, is what you do about them.

CHAPTER 13

ACCELERATING DECISIONS

Organizations can accelerate the flow of information through the business or push power to the edges.

Field Marshal Helmuth Karl Bernhard Graf von Moltke was the brains of the Prussian military for nearly 30 years in the second half of the 19th century. A true Renaissance man, he wrote fiction, travel and history books, translated others' works (he knew seven languages), drew and painted. All this as well as a career in the military so successful that he was handed his title (Graf/Count), made a member of parliament, and had a bridge named in his honour.

During his time in the military, Moltke wrote about strategy, leaving us with two of the most famous quotes on the subject. The first is frequently paraphrased as "No plan survives contact with the enemy." The second, "Strategy is a system of expedients."

It is easier to understand the second quote if you read the full thing:

"Strategy is a system of expedients; it is more than a mere scholarly discipline. It is the translation of knowledge to practical life, the improvement of the original leading thought in accordance with continually changing situations."[37]

What this says to me is that Moltke was an early proponent of agile thinking. He is saying that no strategy, however well considered and prepared, can completely define your future actions, only your intentions. You must constantly adjust your plan of action based on the realities you face at each moment. This seems incredibly apt for today's environment of high frequency change.

Moltke's words support my arguments in the last two chapters; that we need to be much better at understanding the environment we are operating in, remaining close to customers, partners and other stakeholders and picking up signals to steer our behaviour. And that we need to ensure we have solid tools for constantly reassessing our direction over the near term. But they also make it clear that it is not enough to just be a good listener; we need to be able to act on what we hear, at speed.

In Chapter 11, I talked about pushing decisions to the edge of the organization, but sometimes you have to steer the whole organization and it is hard to do that from the edges. Even with an organization appropriately structured to be more athletic, as described in the next chapter, there needs to be a creative, strategic force at the core.

This force, whatever form it takes, whether an individual or more likely a group, needs three things:

- **Information**: Clear, reliable and rich information about the organization's state and operations, as fresh and undoctored as possible, with real-time information being the goal.
- **Culture**: An expectation that radical action will be more frequently required, the will to make radical decisions, and the backing of stakeholders and an organizational culture to do so.
- **Communication**: A method for clearly communicating strategic decisions to colleagues, customers, partners and stakeholders.

INFORMATION

Human beings are sorters by nature. You would not know it by looking at the state of my children's bedrooms, or my workshop, but we like order. We like to categorize and arrange. Sometimes this exercise is valuable, a means of understanding the world. Sometimes it is just a refusal to admit defeat: we sort endlessly in search of a pattern we do not really understand.

Many organizations and their leaders have been seduced by the idea of 'big data' or rather the version of it heavily sold by parts of the tech industry. Their message has been that there is inherent value in large datasets, as long as you can gather them at sufficient scale and order them in a way that they can be properly analysed.

In my experience, this has rarely been the case. Most often, value comes from data when the process starts with a question, not the assembly of an endless set of possible answers. Big data projects are all too often people succumbing to their innate desire to try to order the world, rather than understanding which questions this data might actually answer and what value these answers might carry.

In an athletic organization, leaders do not need to have enormous lakes of data which can be as much of an encumbrance as anything else, with all of the regulations attached to their protection, management and use. Instead they need the tools to answer business questions. That is not just about technology, though software tools and the hardware to power them play an important part. It is about the curiosity and the learned skill to construct the right questions, and the resources to access the data required to answer them if it is not readily available.

So many times, I have seen organizations invest huge sums in collating and ordering their data, but nowhere near enough in equipping their people to use it. Reverse this process: teach people to ask good questions and give them the tools to find answers. Then, and only then, begin to collate the data they need. Do it piece by piece, question by question, but in a consistent framework. This way you will deliver short-term results from the exercise but also create a long-term resource.

CULTURE

Much has been written about a culture of change, though little of it seems to surpass the level of a LinkedIn post in terms of its depth of wisdom. How do you build and maintain a culture in an organization that is based on uncertainty and constant change? Is it even possible, or desirable?

I do not know that it is. At least, I do not think whole organizations can operate like this. Certainly, not the large ones. Think about the communication overhead of constantly steering a whole organization in new directions. Think about how much time is spent in consultation, workshops and feedback sessions during large-scale change events. If you tried to execute that scale of communication across the organization, let alone the other disruptions that change might bring, on a constant basis, you would rapidly destroy the organization and give its people serious mental health issues.

As I'll show in the next chapter, athletic organizations are made up of networks of smaller organizations. Rather than building a culture of change across the whole enterprise, we need to structure businesses for change and ensure that their leaders have the tools at their disposal to make that change when the time comes.

This does not eliminate the need for a culture of change, but it does limit its domain. Rather than a single, organization-spanning culture, the network model described in the next chapter accommodates many different cultures under the same umbrella. Only the culture of change in leadership and its critical stakeholders needs to be considered as an enabler of more rapid decision-making.

These stakeholders will be crucial though. Boards are often natural enemies of radical change, particularly in listed companies where the established business model is continuing to deliver returns. It is a brave chief executive who argues for wholesale change while this is the case. But waiting until the inevitable decline may be too late. As noted earlier, we need to establish whether we are in the business of short-term returns or stewardship. Only organizations where both the leadership and the key stakeholders share a culture of stewardship can be truly athletic.

COMMUNICATION

Where so much of strategy breaks down is in its communication. As discussed in Chapter 8, many strategic decisions do not even make it as far as the annual budget, let alone to the wider ranks of people who must implement them.

Much has been said about the power of storytelling in recent years. It has become quite the fad, a favourite subject of Forbes contributors and TEDx speakers. As is so often the case with these fads, there is a fundamental truth at the heart of the hype, about the narrative structure of stories and how humans respond to them. An understanding of the basic narrative form and ensuring that all of its components are included in the communication of any strategic decision, is an increasingly critical skill for leaders looking to steer organizations more quickly.

I have spent a lot of my career telling stories. Having studied Mechatronic engineering (mechanical and electronic engineering, plus some computer science and management) I took my first job in a marketing agency for technology companies. My employers quickly realized I could speak to engineers on their terms, and I could write in a form that businesspeople understood. I became a translator between the techies, the salespeople and the customers, taking information and turning it into stories that could be sold.

The first thing to consider when building a story is the audience. Every audience you may be speaking to – shareholders or stakeholders, staff, partners or customers

– has a different set of priorities. Every story needs to be tailored to that audience, their needs, their fears. Even this basic step is often missed, with stories solely focused on shareholders or full of jargon that only peers in the sector will understand.

Then there is the narrative form: context, jeopardy, resolution. Where you are today, why you need to move, and what that movement will look like. Critical in the resolution is describing the impact: How will the audience you are speaking to be affected? What role will they play in the resolution? These are simple things, but they are so often overlooked. Telling stories powerfully is an important way to ensure that strategic decisions are acted upon with speed.

DISTRIBUTED INNOVATION

Much of this theory is based on the understanding that radical changes will be needed at some point – in fact, with increasing frequency. But some organizations are taking a different approach, or perhaps a complementary one, trying to ensure that change is truly continuous. Few organizations I have dealt with have a consistent process for innovation across the business. Most are capable of developing new products and services, or delivering occasional improvements in narrow functions, but it is something altogether different to consider innovation across the board in a holistic fashion.

The housing association, Bromford, is one of the exceptions. Here a full-time innovation team constantly prototypes, tests and rolls out new ideas gathered from across the organization. Critically, those examining the value case and success of prototypes are separated from those doing the development, allowing much more rigorous and continuous assessment of the value of each project. Support from the board ensures a small but continuous flow of funds to keep the efforts moving.

Bromford has not totally avoided the need for radical change. It has gone through two mergers in quick succession, becoming an even larger organization. But there is a culture and a practice of continuous change that should minimize the risks of unnecessary radical change to technology, process or structure down the line.

CHAPTER 14

FIT FOR ACTION

It is Christmas time, and your child is obsessed with Ferraris. What toy is going to give them the most joy? A die-cast model Enzo or Testarossa? Or the same car made from Lego?

The die-cast car is the most perfect representation of your child's obsession. You might say it is optimal: all the same sleek lines. But it has a problem: kids get bored quickly. They move on. And the die-cast car? Well, its form is set.

The Lego car, on the other hand, is far from optimal. It has knobbly-bobbly bits all over it. It will never be a perfect representation of the car your child loves. But it has one huge advantage: when they are bored of toy cars it can be a dragon or a dinosaur, a unicorn or a spaceship.

This is not the start of a marketing campaign for Lego. It is an allegory for modern business. Because I think we have spent a hundred years learning how to build businesses like die-cast cars. And in just a few short years, we must learn to build them like Lego.

ADAPTATION VS OPTIMIZATION

The critical description of that die-cast model is 'optimal'. It is a perfect representation of the larger model it is trying to represent. As I noted in Chapter 8, most business theory and practice are about optimization. It is about doing what we do, better, where better usually means cheaper, quicker, with less waste and ultimately more profit. Having this as the core objective for leadership is valid when your business model might sustain for decades. It is less appropriate in an age where your business model might have a lifespan measured in months.

So, what is the alternative? You build your business for adaptation. You build it out of Lego bricks, rather than die-cast steel. You accept the overhead of knobbly-bobbly bits in return for more sustainable success rather than a much shorter, albeit more profitable lifespan.

STOP TALKING

About 2002, Jeff Bezos sent out a memo to the staff of Amazon. Actually, it was described by Steve Yegge as a 'mandate', and it was one of many. Yegge is an engineer who worked at Amazon, then Google, and who hit the headlines in 2018 for leaving Google, criticizing its failure to innovate. Yegge first achieved widespread notoriety in 2011 when he published a ranting memo of his own, comparing the strengths and weaknesses of these two tech giants.[38] It was meant to go only to colleagues in Google but Yegge, using the unfamiliar Google+ social network, made it public. In the post, Yegge referred to the memo from Bezos.

Bezos is a famously strict micromanager. But this mandate stood out because in Yegge's words it was "so out there, so huge and eye-bulgingly ponderous." The contents of the memo were pretty technical but let me give you the summary. It said: "Stop talking to each other."

In your typical large organization, a lot of the work gets done by human-to-human interaction, one way or another. Sometimes these conversations, face-to-face, by phone or by email, are critical. They are the source of creativity, relationships and collaboration. But they also have their downsides. Processes built on human relationships are often opaque, inconsistent and hard to maintain. Most of all, they are inflexible: they are the basis of the die-cast model described above. What Bezos seems to have wanted more than anything is flexibility.

Bezos demanded that every function of the business be wrapped in a layer of software that exposed what it did to everyone else. All interactions between these functions would happen through the software, not through emails, calls or conversations. With just a simple line of code you could now see a menu of everything a function like finance or IT could provide. With another you could find out what inputs that function required in order to return a result. Just a few lines of script could build up an automatic inter-action between one function and another. You could keep going, assembling different functions until you assembled a complete business.

This software interface is the digital equivalent of Lego's knobbly-bobbly bits. With one memo, albeit followed by years of work under threat of losing your job if it was not done, Jeff Bezos transformed Amazon from a die-cast toy car into a box of Lego bricks.

The result is that Amazon is perhaps the most agile com-pany in the world now. If Amazon wants to launch a new ser-vice, it is a question of assembling some of its existing bricks and adding a new thin layer on top. If it does not work, it can just roll up that single layer: the rest of the infrastructure is still supporting other parts of the organization.

Amazon now has one of the most sustainable sources of income because it is not only Amazon that makes things with the bricks that Bezos' memo created. Amazon Web Services, the wrapper for a selection of the bricks, now accounts for almost half of the public cloud computing market, making Amazon $6bn per quarter. A huge pro-portion of the websites and apps that you use are hosted on Amazon's infrastructure. Companies around the world access these services in just the same way that other functions inside Amazon do. They can take the building blocks that Amazon has created and use them in their own organization: a few lines of code here and there and your systems can talk directly to Amazon's, integrating seamlessly as if they were your own.

Whole businesses are now being built using Amazon's systems, including the armies of micro-businesses that make up a lot of Amazon's logistics arm. Here Amazon has provided individuals and small fleets with the building blocks of software to run their own businesses. All you need is a van and you can be a remote part of the Amazon empire.

IT'S ALL ABOUT FRICTION

The critical point here is about friction. Amazon has created a low-friction, digital way to access all its functions, not just the services that were traditionally customer-facing. Assembling a business like this undoubtedly has overheads but, by keeping the friction low, Amazon makes them manageable and accepts the trade-off of efficiency against adaptability.

Not everyone can do what Amazon did. Not everyone can become a service provider to other businesses on this scale. But the point of this brick-based business architecture is that not everyone has to. Some businesses will be an agglomeration of bricks, some might be just one. Some organizations might be net consumers of other people's services, others might be net suppliers. The point is that we can assemble and reconfigure services at an incredible rate with this approach.

So how do you go about breaking a business down into bricks?

Here the building block analogy is also useful. Every brick has a function and two interfaces: inputs and outputs. How many inputs and outputs will depend on how granular you want to make the division between functions. They might be high level: finance, HR, logistics. They might be much more specific: accounts receivable, employee onboarding, warehouse inventory. What is critical is not so much what sits inside the unit, but how clearly its capabilities are communicated. How accessible its services are made. And how transparent it is about its performance.

TRANSPARENCY

One of the most terrifying things I found when I started consulting with large organizations was just how opaque they were to senior leadership. I found that many people at the top of organizations lacked a real understanding of the performance of some critical functions. They did not have the knowledge or the time to scrutinize them, nor the right headline metrics to benchmark their performance.

In many ways this is a problem of expectation. In a deeply-integrated company – the die-cast model – there is simply too much to observe, too many close connections to monitor.

It is overwhelming and there is no obvious place to start with a deeper examination. Most leaders are, in my experience, firefighting constantly, bouncing from one function's issues to another. In what you might call the network model, assembled from bricks, most functions of the business are at one remove. This less direct, more distant connection enforces two things. Firstly, you must allow the functional unit a greater level of autonomy. Operating at one remove, it needs to be self-sufficient. The leader's job becomes about composing services from the blocks available, or commissioning new ones, rather than micromanaging the minutiae of each one.

Secondly, when instituting a network model, you have to put some metrics in place to track the performance of each functional unit. These metrics in integrated businesses are often missing, or ill-thought-out, leading to perverse incentives. The classic example is procurement teams being incentivized on purchase price rather than on lifetime value. The result is often substandard goods that have to be replaced more frequently, ultimately costing more. These issues can be surprisingly invisible, or intractable, inside an integrated business because on paper the function in question is performing well. Such issues are often more carefully examined in outsourced arrangements. The process of commissioning such contracts naturally inspires a greater degree of consideration from lawyers keen to avoid loopholes through which suppliers might extract excess profits.

There is no guarantee that the metrics are better chosen or measured in a network model, but there are opportunities to institute them in the transition process, which is not unlike the outsourcing process. When procuring external bricks to build your business from, you can select them based on those with robust metrics. And when converting internal functions to the new model, wrapping them in a clear interface, there is a great opportunity to institute metrics and make them the responsibility of the person with the delegated power.

DIFFICULT DECISIONS

So far, so positive, but there is a ruthless aspect to this model as well: sometimes old bricks are no longer needed in the new design. This network model is explicitly designed to allow the organization as a whole to be more resilient, but sometimes that will mean sacrificing individual components.

Those people to whom you have delegated power, semi-autonomous control of a whole function, may find themselves cut adrift from the wider organization. But there is light at the end of this tunnel. Firstly, this excision might save the host, making everyone else's jobs more secure. But secondly, the excised function is well set up to be able to engage elsewhere. In fact, the most successful functions may already have client bases beyond the original host. To some extent their destiny is in their own hands, given the right supporting framework.

ASSEMBLING BRICKS

Collections of bricks can be assembled in any number of ways but working with clients I designed a model that has proven to be useful on more than one occasion. This is a model of layers.

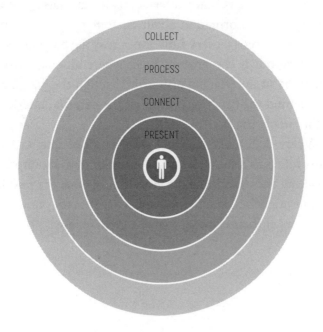

THE STRATIFICATION LAYER DIAGRAM

Imagine a series of concentric circles. At the centre is the customer, and wrapped around them, a single, coherent interface layer. This represents all the means by which customer and organization communicate into a single set of touchpoints with common design, language and standards. This might all be owned by the organization or there might be partners in this layer.

Behind the customer interface is a data layer, a consistent set of information about customers, products and suppliers shared by every function across the business. The next ring out is the process layer, where all your critical functions sit, interfacing primarily through the data layer. And behind the functional layer sit the external interfaces to the supply chain.

Where does leadership sit? Outside all of this. Leadership's role is as a composer and controller now, monitoring, tweaking and examining the evidence for what the next big change might be, clear in the knowledge that they now have the levers at their disposal to make great change.

ISN'T TALKING VALUABLE?

Perhaps the most consistent criticism of this approach is that it creates new silos, isolating people from different disciplines instead of bringing them together to innovate and collaborate. My answer comes in the form of a question: How often do your people do that today? How often do they have the time and energy to spontaneously collaborate to improve the business? The answer is 'frequently' in only a vanishingly small number of organizations.

Rather, it is a leader's role to make space for collaboration and innovation. To formalize spaces where people can come together to address what is next. This is no harder in a network model than in a monolithic die-cast. If anything, the revised structure coupled with increased delegation should create more space and time for thinking about change.

CHAPTER 15

THE OPPOSITE OF AGILE

Our political systems are not in any way athletic. Quite the opposite. Our companies and public bodies are not, for the most part, athletic. How athletic are we as individuals? There is an argument that some of the recent wave of populism around the world could be put down to intransigence. Just look at the characteristics of swathes of the Trump supporting base or Brexit voter. These are movements that span many different generations and social groups, otherwise they would not have been as successful as they have. But at the core of both is a group of disenfranchised older men who feel as if the world has moved on and they have been left behind.[39] Their votes are as much about resisting this change as anything else.

Even if we are neophiles by nature, thrilled by the new, much of the change we perceive carries a threat to our status, to our very understanding of the world. Many of us would rather reject it and push for a return to some mythical past than to grab the future with both hands. Change will always come by generations and we can see that driven by economic and social factors; the 'millennials' (now mostly in their thirties) and their successors may behave differently. They are native in the increasingly digital world that remains a place their parents only visit, and they have grown up with the fast-paced change that it enables. They are at least somewhat adapted to being surrounded by noise and having to pick the signal from it. Their formative years were spent moving rapidly between trends, seeing fashion change six, ten or twelve times a year in the shops, bands come and go. They have learned to navigate a library of 30 million songs on the celestial jukebox, celebrating music's ephemerality rather than losing themselves in a single album for weeks. They consume shorter bites of content on YouTube, choose short-lease apartments so as not to be tied down[40] and to account for the perceived insecurity in their work.[41] Perhaps, generation by generation, we will adapt.

This process will happen naturally. But our organizations will not change on their own, particularly our political structures.

Political power in the UK is hyper-centralized.[42] Control of both tax and spending is concentrated strongly with central government rather than federated to the regions. In the US, power is more distributed, but perhaps still too weighted towards the centre. The network model, this is not, and the die-cast nature of our institutions is showing. Under stress they have demonstrated that they are extremely linear, only able to process issues in serial fashion. And they are deeply disconnected from the citizen, with frustration at this perceived distance being another factor driving the Brexit and Trump votes.

Devolution has begun in the UK, but it probably needs to travel a lot further in order to address these challenges. Powers over taxes, as well as spending, will need to be pushed to cities and regions. But we should be clear up front that this will lead to the very definition of a postcode lottery. There will be winners and losers. But this is better than the alternative: whole countries being bound to the past by the sclerotic decision-making at the core.

Where this book is most focused though is on less ancient institutions more capable of change. Public, private or third sector, all our organizations need to change in order to adapt to this new age of high frequency change, if there is any ambition among their leaders to deliver sustainable success rather than short-term returns.

Most fundamentally, we need to look at how our organizations are structured. I simply do not believe that monolithic enterprises held together with creaking processes and the blood, sweat and tears of a few good people overexerting themselves are sustainable models for the future. We need to transform our organizations into networks of semi-autonomous units, with power and control devolved, including a degree of power over their own destiny. We should end the pretence that we can maintain a single corporate culture across organizations of hundreds or thousands of people. It is not even clear to me that this is a desirable objective, as long as there is coherence and consistency in the customer experience

The successful organizations of tomorrow will be loosely-coupled networks of components, some owned, some outsourced and accessed through low-friction, largely digital, interfaces. At the heart of these organizations will be teams of strategic thinkers and operations experts, coordinating the different components and keeping a watchful eye on the next trends.

PART 3

THE
HUMAN
RESPONSE

CHAPTER 16

LIFE IN A HIGH FREQUENCY FUTURE

For a while I had a running conversation with the TV presenter, Tim Lovejoy. It started when I went on his weekend magazine show, *Sunday Brunch*, and ended up discussing the future, jobs, religion and climate change with Tim, his co-host, and a variety of celebrity guests. It continued in the pub when he came to host an event I was running in Manchester. And it was one of the main subjects when I appeared on his podcast. The topic was one that has become a running theme for me, the basis of many questions following talks and after-dinner speeches: What will we do in the future?

The question is, in part, spurred by the reality of high frequency change, and what it implies for our working lives particularly. We have largely accepted now that the job for life of old is gone. So long gone in fact that I probably must explain to younger readers (born after about 1990) that in the past people usually worked for a single employer their entire lives and retired on a solid pension built up over years of service. This seems strange in a world where the average tenure in a role is just five years.[43]

High frequency change threatens to shorten that tenure, particularly if you are working in one of the organizations that does not prepare for it. The company you are working for might fail, undermined by an unforeseen shift in trends. Or the role you have might become obsolete because of a change in technology, requiring you to retrain into a new role more frequently than in the past.

These effects will not hit every sector or every organization simultaneously, but it seems likely that people will be required to change roles more often. And that offers a second threat: if employees are spending less than five years on average with an employer, how much will the employers be willing to invest in them?

The idea of a 'job' implies more than work. It is a social contract as much as a financial one between employer and employee. In return for the employee's commitment, the employer will develop them in their role and help to make provisions for their future, through a pension. At least that is what a job used to mean. But, according to government figures,[44] already today more than a third of employers offer their staff no training or development opportunities.

SEX AND RELATIONSHIPS

The last few years has seen a general loosening of the bond between employer and employee. There was the expansion of zero-hour contracts. The challenge of the 'self-employed' nature of Uber drivers and other 'gig economy' workers, who sometimes appear to be required to behave like employees but without any of the protection that implies under law. This trend is unlikely to reverse, even if there are policy interventions and legal challenges to slow its progress. Employees represent risk for a business that acknowledges it might have to change direction fast, as well as costing the company more than their freelance equivalents. In any role where long-term demand is uncertain, companies will do what they can to minimize their exposure to cost and risk.

This may seem counterproductive in the long term. Surely you want workers who are committed to your success? Willing to go the extra mile for the business? This is surely true of workers in some roles, but in many positions humans are only placeholders for the incoming robots. In these positions it is very hard to see why employers would choose to invest more than what is absolutely necessary. As someone described it to me recently, companies are more interested in sex than relationships. They want instant gratification from their employees, not an extended partnership based on shared values and mutual respect.

RISE OF THE ROBOTS

As noted in Chapter 4, throughout evolution, going back at least 3.5 million years, we have used tools to amplify our own capabilities. The coming wave of automation must be seen in that light. In the current economic system, it is inevitable that we will apply the technology we have created in order to lower the friction in our organizations. And lower friction means fewer humans.

Estimates for how many people could be displaced from the workforce by automation vary. The most aggressive estimates, such as those from the Oxford Martin School at the University of Oxford, a multidisciplinary unit addressing global challenges, suggest that 47% of roles could be automated.[45] It is crucial to note that the authors of this paper are not saying that 47% of jobs 'will' be automated, but that they are 'exposed' to the risk of automation. My contention is that many jobs that are exposed will be automated because of the economic incentives for businesses to do so.

Incidentally, the Oxford Martin figure aligns quite well with a figure from the research of David Graeber, professor of anthropology at the London School of Economics. According to Graeber's study of 'bullshit jobs', about 40% of people believe their work adds no real value.[46] Maybe they are right.

Other estimates for the number of jobs to be affected by automation range from as low as 9%,[47] with most figures from the OECD (14%),[48] McKinsey (15%)[49] and PwC (30%)[50] somewhere in between. Each uses a somewhat different methodology, and each comes to different conclusions about the jobs that technology will create while it destroys others. I am largely pessimistic about the prospect for jobs in the face of automation. It is hard to see how much of the new work that might be created is not also taken by machines. Certainly, I believe there is a good chance that 14-15% of jobs could go and not be replaced by other jobs with anything like the same security.

Machines in the past have only been able to enhance, or outright surpass, our physical capabilities. Today they are challenging us for cognitive roles. This does not mean machines can think like us: they are nowhere near that level of capability. But they do not have to be. Most humans perform at a fraction of their potential for most of the working day. Machines only need to be able to match that fraction of human performance in order to be able to take a large percentage of the work. Anywhere that the work can be codified by rules that do not change for a reasonable period of time, whether that is processing paperwork in an office, interfacing with customers in a call centre, driving a taxi, moving crates or making products, machines will take a growing proportion of roles.

What many humans will be left with is not jobs, but work. Piecemeal tasks that machines cannot do because they lack our flexibility, originality and empathy. Some of these tasks will be very rewarding, and some less so: the physical flexibility of human beings is still something that is very expensive to replicate mechanically. There will remain dangerous and dirty jobs that can be most cheaply completed by a human worker.

In an ideal world we would revalue some of the most uniquely human work, currently desperately undervalued, like teaching, nursing and care. But there is little sign that this is happening in the current environment of squeezed public spending. To do so would require an increase in taxation, or a dramatic reprioritization of spending.

THE GAPS BETWEEN

My hypothesis then is that a larger and larger proportion of the population will be essentially freelance – already one of the fastest growing categories of work in both the US[51] and UK.[52] Some people will still be employed in a classic job, but these will be people who spend a larger fraction of their day completing uniquely human tasks. The threshold may only be 5% – in other words you may only need to be performing at a high level for half an hour a day for it to make sense for an employer to want to pay you full time rather than piecemeal. But this still leaves a huge number of people as part of a much more fluid workforce.

Because of the size of this workforce and the lower availability of work – it is hard to see how anything close to full employment remains possible – people are likely to have some periods where they are juggling multiple engagements, and others where they are between work. I think it is very likely that people will increasingly develop 'side hustles'; interest, family or community-based work that returns value in cash, tax relief or in kind.

In fallow periods, how will people fill their time? I believe education has a huge role to play.

AN END NOT (JUST) A MEANS

The next few chapters are largely about a set of skills that will best equip people for the workforce in a world of high frequency change. But it is important to acknowledge that education is not just a means to an end, a tool for equipping the workforce. It is an end in itself. Maslow's Hierarchy of Needs may be a rather limited model of human behaviour, but it is hard to argue with what is at the top. Once our basic needs are fulfilled, we chase self-actualization and self-improvement. Growing our own understanding, developing our skills, or expanding the sum of human knowledge, need to be recognized as valuable goals for someone to pursue, and we probably need to support people while they are doing it.

While people are unemployed, they will need financial support to maintain their basic needs. But people also need purpose. Side by side studies of communities in poverty show much higher propensity for crime and anti-social behaviour in those where people lack purpose. Anecdotally, it is clear that even with wealth, those without purpose are likely to make for poor members of society. Lots of people can find purpose for themselves, but education – of all forms – is a widely shared goal and unalloyed social good. Making further and higher education available, for free, throughout life, would be a very strong policy step to giving us greater resilience in the face of high frequency change.

UNIVERSAL BASIC INCOME

There remains the question, however, of how people are financially supported when there is no work to support them. The idea of a universal basic income (UBI), a constant benefit given to everyone, in or out of work, without means testing, has many supporters from the world of technology. It is an attractive idea because it allows us to maintain the current economic system, driven by consumer spending, without contemplating larger changes. Put money in people's pockets and they will keep putting it through the tills, and the world keeps turning.

The idea has common sense appeal, but even before we get to the question of how it is paid for, there are practical challenges. The current benefits system in the UK, for all its weaknesses, is targeted to address specific disadvantages. It is designed to provide, even if it is not effective at delivering, something of an equalizing effect. A UBI would likely wipe out a lot of the means-tested benefits, since one of the arguments for it is that the administration of means-testing wastes a lot of money that could be better handed direct to citizens.

The other major issue is how large a UBI should be. Imagine it was at the level of the basic UK state pension (roughly £6,500 a year) and given without limitation to everyone between the ages of 16 and 64 – roughly 60% of the population. Before you look at taxing some of that back, that is about £260 billion, slightly more than the current total welfare budget. On top of this, you would have to add the current pension bill (around £110 billion) and likely many measures of additional support for those with various forms of disability or incapacity (up to another £40 billion). If you were to offset this by taxing some of the UBI back, you would have difficult questions to answer about what level of earnings people would require before this tax kicks in. You cannot tax back their earnings up to the level of the UBI, or you would risk creating a serious disincentive to work for the lowest paid – particularly those who would need to pay for childcare in order to work. So at what level does it kick in? Bear in mind two thirds of the working population earn less than £50,000 per year, so any tax that would recoup a significant proportion of the UBI would have to kick in below that level.

In short, even giving people just £125 a week would require massive tax increases or dramatic cuts in other areas of government spending. To give them something like the living wage – three times as much as the state pension – would require a wholesale change in our expectations about levels of tax.

ROBOT TAX

One of the oft-proposed answers to this conundrum is a so-called robot tax. If companies are replacing people with machines, then the argument goes that we should tax the machines. This idea is an absolute non-starter, rooted in a total lack of understanding of the nature of the machines that will be taking people's jobs. It presumes that someone can both quantify and qualify the machines: count them and sort them into categories, since you would assume that they will have different tax bands based on their scale and function. A machine that takes 25% of someone's job must be taxed differently to one that takes 100%. But who would know the difference? These machines will be largely invisible, and ephemeral: an algorithm will spin up for a few fractions of a second on a server on the other side of the world, someplace where energy and bandwidth are cheap. It will fulfil its task and then fade away into memory before its identical twin appears a few microseconds later to serve a different customer elsewhere. These are not spinning jennies or even self-driving cars, for the most part. Even the software companies that sell them will struggle to count them, as they do today: it is a constant battle for the likes of Microsoft to accurately count and charge for the software licences it has sold.

The only realistic option is to get a better grip on corporation tax. To tax the inevitably larger profits that corporations can make when they replace people with machines. That requires international cooperation to avoid companies just moving their revenues around to the lowest tax domain. And international cooperation is under a lot of pressure right now.

PROSPECTS FOR SUCCESS

Among this change and turmoil, there will still be a strong role for human beings. In the workplace, in the jobs that persist, and as freelancers, there will be a particular set of uniquely human skills that are valued. Skills that help organizations to be more adaptable, and skills that help individuals to sell their role in others' success. These skills can be grouped under three headings: Curation, Creativity and Communication.

CHAPTER 17

CURATION

One of the most vaunted skills of computers is their ability to process large data sets and extract meaning: 'machine learning' from 'big data'. But machines can only handle the data they are fed. They cannot identify gaps in that data, alternative sources or determine criteria for assessing its veracity.

Human beings can be much more flexible and interrogative of information, recognizing gaps in what is available and sourcing information to fill those gaps. Humans can learn to validate sources against one another and test them against basic truths. They can develop heuristics – rules of thumb – to help them sniff out false from true. These are the new skills of curation: recognizing gaps, sourcing information to fill them, and qualifying what is found.

This is a slightly different use of the word curation to the way it may be used in the context of content marketing or an art gallery or a museum. There the challenge is one of assembling narrative or coherence from a range of artefacts. Here it is rather broader, but the match in meaning is close enough to be a useful headline for this group of skills, especially since it allows me to call them the 'Three Cs'.

Curation skills can really be broken down into two categories or stages: discovery and qualification.

DISCOVERY

Discovery is about knowing how to ask the right questions in a range of contexts. It is about the ability to identify a problem and, even from a very small knowledge base, begin exploring it until you can start to find a solution.

This is challenging when facing a completely new problem, because you often do not have the language with which to shape the question. Likewise, the language in which the answer is returned may be totally unfamiliar. But through an iterative process of asking questions, absorbing answers, and using the new knowledge to ask better questions, you can begin to explore.

A great example of this skill in action today can be seen by watching someone who is skilled at constructing search engine queries. The first place most of us turn for an answer these days is to a search engine. But how do you formulate the question to find the answer you need if you are exploring something completely new? You start with your best-guess approximation, learn from what it returns, and progressively refine until you find the answer. Skilled users of Google, Bing and the other search engines are fascinating to watch in these circumstances, rapidly tapping out queries using the system's various filters, scanning what they find, and returning to the search bar with a revised query that gets them closer to their goal.

These people are comfortable with ignorance, knowing it is a state that has a very limited term. It can be eradicated with just a few keystrokes. In an age of high frequency change we will all need to become comfortable with ignorance and skilled in the tools to overcome it. The compressed and connected nature of our world means there will be an ever-growing array of ideas we are unfamiliar with. The turnover of these ideas will continue to accelerate as they are constantly refreshed and supplemented. We can never know them all. In fact, we will die still ignorant of most. But we can live with this if we know that we can find the ideas and information we need, when we need them.

QUALIFICATION

When you find an answer – a piece of information – then the skills of qualification kick in. How do you know you can trust what you have found? Too often people take what they have read on face value and compound the error or untruth by sharing it on, passing it unfiltered into the business or into their own social networks. The skills of qualification are about building tests in your own mind based on your existing knowledge and what you can glean from other sources around the topic you are examining.

Over time people can build up a good nose for right and wrong. A sixth sense for truth that makes inaccuracies just 'feel' wrong. This might be based on acquired knowledge of a particular field. It can be enhanced by simple tests: a quick bit of maths can often tell you that a reported number must be false. But sometimes qualification can only come through rigour and discipline, double and triple-checking with reliable sources.

The last few years have demonstrated the importance of this skill of qualification. We have witnessed naked untruths being distributed around social networks and the internet to incredible effect. We have running battles over divisive issues, particularly around identity, with both sides claiming the primacy of their facts. And we have people in power willing to brazenly deny the truth. If this were not enough, we are on the verge of a new wave of technologies being widely available that will make fake news and reality even harder to distinguish from one another.

Audio and video editing tools will soon allow the construction of entirely fake clips with just a few samples of the real thing. We've already seen examples of off-the-shelf, even free, computing tools being used to create fake pornography, with the faces of famous actresses appended to the bodies of other performers. This required some talent but soon the tools will be ubiquitous. It won't take some special effects expert in Hollywood to create a believable fake. Anyone will be able to do it, on their home computer or even phone. These fake clips will be near-indistinguishable from the real thing. They will undoubtedly be weaponized by a whole variety of bad actors. The only defence against them will be the skills of sceptical enquiry, drawing on multiple evidence sources to separate false from true.

Given the accessibility of such technology, it is important to retain a degree of open-mindedness as well. Whether political, personal or professional, we are all subject to confirmation bias. We will not automatically challenge evidence supporting our own views with the same rigour we might apply to that which contradicts them.

SELF-DIRECTED LEARNING

Perhaps the most important area we must curate is our own knowledge and skills. Much of the information we acquire at school will be out of date by the time we reach the workplace, whether that is in science, geography or perhaps even language, given the speed at which it seems to be changing in a globally-connected culture. Likewise, the technical skills we learn at the start of our careers are unlikely to stand us in good stead for the rest of our working lives. We will have to constantly reassess our capabilities and retrain ourselves for the next leg of our career.

This turnover of skills, and need for a constant return to learning, may have serious impacts on the further and higher education sectors over the next few decades. It is hard to see how the standard three-year undergraduate degree remains relevant in this context. No, education clearly is not all about your ability to work, as I note in Chapter 16. And it is likely that many who can afford to will still choose to soft launch their adult lives at a university. But for many in the future it may seem like an indulgence, giving up a three-year head start to your future peers in the workplace.

Instead people will choose to learn when their career either affords it or requires it. That may be a fallow period between jobs. It may be the luxury of a career break. Or it may be when they have hit a glass ceiling they cannot shatter without additional qualifications.

How people pay for this is an interesting question. One alternative idea put to me by John Chapman, the editorial director of technology magazine *IT Europa*, was to give everyone a lump sum at birth to be spent on education throughout their lives. Any time they needed to enter education, the grant could be tapped for their fees. This would clearly have tax implications for the wider public, but given the growing need for all of us to skill, and reskill, and the potential for us to need useful engagement between periods of work, it certainly has its merits.

ENGINES OF DISCOVERY

A world filled with constant change means we will all be constantly seeking the new, for fun, fulfilment or competitive advantage. And the level of noise in that world will require us to learn to filter effectively, finding the signal and ensuring its veracity. Most fundamentally, we need to be able to identify gaps and shape the questions to fill them, particularly where those gaps are in our own knowledge and skills and presenting barriers to our own advancement.

CHAPTER 18

CREATIVITY

A BBC report on secondary education in the UK in 2018 showed that nine out of every ten schools had cut back on lesson time, staff or facilities in at least one creative arts subject.[53] Unsurprisingly, this is reflected in the number of students taking such classes, which fell more than 20% between 2010 and 2017.[54] The response from the chief of the education regulator, Ofsted, was that 'academic subjects' were the best route to higher level study, especially for working class children (if this was Twitter, not a book, I would insert an 'eye roll' emoji here). The picture is similar in the United States, where two thirds of teachers say creative subjects are being crowded out of the curriculum.[55]

All of this took place during an extended period of focus on the idea of a 'knowledge economy'. This was one of the motivators behind the growing prioritization of 'core' subjects in education, and in the UK, a return to some rote learning of facts that had been largely stripped from the curriculum in favour of more focus on application and critical thought.

I find fault with just about all of this: the dismissal of creative subjects as not being 'academic', the idea that they are somehow less valuable as people continue in education or work, that rote learning of knowledge is valuable, or that there is even such a thing as a knowledge economy in the future.

THE NONSENSE OF THE KNOWLEDGE ECONOMY

When politicians talk about a 'knowledge economy', it sounds like information is gold. A durable good that can be stored and trickled out to the market to keep its value high.

It is not.

Just a couple of decades ago, it might have been true. If you came up with a new product, process or business model, you probably had a few years grace before it was replicated. With the wind behind you, you could create a defensible position, for a while at least.

In an age of high frequency change, this is no longer true.

Knowledge is not durable like gold. It is a fast-moving consumer good. A low-value, high-volume commodity. The power in knowledge today is not in holding it but in managing its flow. Getting it into your business quickly, extracting its value and moving on. The value of the knowledge at the heart of every business is constantly being eroded. The gold turned to lead.

The result of this is that rote learning at school age largely embeds knowledge that has completely depreciated by the time you reach the workplace. Yes, it is nice to be able to do multiplication in your head, recall global capitals or recite a poem or two. But those things are best acquired by their application, not by learning them for learning's sake: stored knowledge is a by-product of use, not an end in itself. When the entire sum of the world's knowledge is just a few screen taps or a voice command away, the advantage conferred by stored knowledge is only fractional. When, in just a decade's time, most of us are working through a digital interface augmented with artificial intelligence that can predict our questions and provide facts without even a formal request, that advantage is even smaller.

A SKILLS ECONOMY

The value that humans add in tomorrow's economy comes not from knowledge but skills. In fact, any individual human fulfilment, employed or otherwise, is largely based on acquisition, application and development of skills. We like to be good at things and the process of getting there is incredibly rewarding. It is with these skills that we can process and extract value from future knowledge, critical in a fast-moving economy. Knowledge should be treated in education as a by-product of skills development. Yes, it is important that we have some – even a lot. But its acquisition should not be the goal, because knowledge is highly unlikely to fulfil us or make us more productive members of society. It is skills that do that.

The school curriculum, therefore, should be determined not on which subjects convey the most valuable knowledge, but which provide the optimum opportunities to teach skills. This is where the true value of the creative arts subjects is revealed. While there might be inherent value in exposing people to the joys of art, design, literature, poetry and dance at school, and I would argue there is, what the creative subjects really are is the best venue in which to teach the skills of creativity.

This is the opposite of saying that these are the 'only' subjects where creativity can be applied or taught. Creativity is a critical skill in maths and science, just as much as it is in art or design. In many ways the grouping of arts subjects under the 'creative' banner reinforces this sense that creativity is limited to these domains. But whether you are drawing or painting, writing, composing or choreographing, the creative arts will constantly expose you to the fundamental aspects of creativity, including failure.

ITERATION NOT INSPIRATION

Creativity is perhaps the most misunderstood human skill. We see it as innate, something you either have or do not have, and we connect it too closely to a limited set of its applications. Many people come out of school considering themselves uncreative because they cannot draw or paint. This is sad, and false.

Creativity is primarily a learned skill and, in many ways, it is like the scientific method. It is about applying ideas, seeing them fail and learning from that failure. It is about iteration and recombination much more than it is about inspiration. You only need to see the discarded drafts of the great writers, or the many sketches of the great artists, to know the truth in this. Given the incredible amount of hype around start-ups and their 'fail fast and try again' culture, it is amazing the parallels between the arts subjects and start-up success are not more widely recognized by governments trying to jumpstart their economies.

In an age of high frequency change, where existing products and services are being rapidly devalued, creativity is perhaps the most critical skill in business. It is creativity that latches on to possibilities and turns them into the products and services that will ensure any organization's next wave of success.

If you want to see how critical this is in numeric terms, just look at the accelerating turnover of products, services and companies described in Chapter Two. The collapse in the longevity of successful businesses on the stock market, and the incredible speed at which digital ideas and products can reach a global audience, displacing their predecessors. The only way to counter this is to be constantly creating the next products and services that the world will demand.

A DEFENSIBLE SKILL

Machines can be a great aid to creativity. They can help us to capture ideas, test them, communicate them and translate designs into prototypes and ultimately products. They can even produce original solutions to well-defined problems, given the right inputs. For example, machines already produce thousands, if not millions, of media articles each year, writing stock reports and sports roundups pulling on automated data feeds and running them through processes to wrap that data in language.[56] Machines are starting to produce original designs for physical products too, creating chairs that have the optimum balance of strength, weight and cost, using the minimum amount of material.[57] They have redesigned cars[58] and aircraft components[59] for better performance, and have even had a go at fashion.[60]

But in every case, these machines are working to a brief defined by humans. The creativity is in capturing the right scope and recognizing the right inputs, building an algorithm that delivers realistic results. Even then most of these machines are only returning prototypes for people to test and polish. They are powerful because they can simultaneously account for more variables than a person can hold in their head and explore millions of possibilities beyond human imagination before settling on answers that fit the brief. But ultimately humans are both starting and finishing the process. Creativity remains a defensible human skill in the face of rising automation.

We need to learn to make the most of the augmentation that the next generation of machines offers us. These are the skills we should be teaching in schools now. How to recognize a challenge and theorize a response. How to define the parameters for success and source the required inputs to deliver it. How to leverage the power of machines to augment our creativity, and in the delivery of the final product or service. How to fail and learn from that failure to ensure a better result the second time around. These are the creative skills that a high frequency age requires.

LEARN THROUGH PLAY

In the absence of a shift in the curriculum to support these ends, those of us with the resources to do so will continue to enhance our own education and that of our children beyond the classroom, sadly widening the class divide. How do we do this? In large part, through play.

Hobbies, and particularly creative hobbies, are a fantastic venue in which to practise creative skills. With my children it is everything from the usual messy arts of making through gluing and painting cereal boxes into various shapes and colours, through to coding and even soldering up their own small electronics projects. For me, most recently, it has been learning how to roller skate. This was a painful skill to learn as I approached 40, in more ways than one. I cracked ribs, strained wrists and turned one of my elbows into a squidgy, oversized ball at various points. But perhaps the greater damage, and more valuable learning, was psychological. Learning a hobby later in life is humbling. By our late thirties we are so used to operating in spheres in which we have become expert that we tend to lose a little perspective. Entering a field where you are utterly outperformed by many eight-year-olds is a great reminder of how little you really know.

Learning tricks on roller skates is an iterative process involving a lot of failure – hence the injuries. Given the physical pain, learning to overcome those failures and try again is particularly hard. But it is also incredibly rewarding when you finally land that jump neatly, or learn to spin around without losing momentum.

If you are concerned about your future career, or that of your child, then taking up a new creative hobby is my best prescription. Dedicate yourself to it. Try and try again. Fail and continue. And enjoy the mastery of even the basic skills. Take up the same hobby as your children and be humbled by their ability to learn faster. But ultimately know that everyone is creative, and honing that creative skill is a critical component of being future-ready.

CHAPTER 19

COMMUNICATION

Does an idea have any value if it cannot be shared? This sounds like the old thought experiment about trees falling in forests when no one is around: do they make any sound? But it has a real bearing on why communication is a critical skill for securing work in tomorrow's world.

The high frequency, low friction environment I have described is characterized by an increasingly networked structure to the world, and particularly to business. Very little is done these days by a single organization. We rely on globe spanning networks of suppliers, partners and channels for everything from finance to manufacturing to software systems. Even single organizations are now coming to resemble networks, rather than monoliths, as laid out in Chapter 14.

Networks are made up of nodes and each node has an interface to other nodes. When the network is made up of a small number of large nodes – for example, large corporations – then the amount of communication many of us must do is limited. We can exist happily at the middle of a node, required only to communicate with our immediate colleagues.

As the character of the network changes to one of many more, much smaller nodes, then more of us find ourselves close to, or even at the edge of a node. Now we are the primary interface to other nodes in the network, and our communication workload climbs dramatically. The success of the whole node might come down to our ability to interface with others. The smaller nodes in this scenario range from the functional units – the Lego bricks – described in Chapter 14, through to the rising number of freelance workers we see on both sides of the Atlantic.

Networked businesses change more frequently – that is why they are built as networks. This too raises the importance of communication. As a representative of a small node you will constantly be promoting that node's interests in order to stay engaged with current customers, or to become part of new collaborations. As an individual this workload is even greater: your livelihood depends on it.

Outside this very sales-centric model, the importance of communication and collaboration is growing. Just look at the way software is built today: global shared projects built by whole armies of developers collaborating across companies and continents. Assemblies of existing components ('libraries') and other people's services ('Application Programming Interfaces' or APIs) are wrapped in some original code. There is constant evolution in the libraries as they adapt to new demands and possibilities. Likewise, with the APIs. Modern software is never finished; it is an endlessly evolving ecosystem and its continued success relies on continuing, live partnerships. It requires communication.

Given this importance, what are the critical components of this communication skill?

LISTENING

I have a vivid memory of an outside trainer coming to our school one day to teach a session on life skills. His subject was communication and he asked the entire room what the most important skills of communication were. Not one of us came up with listening. We were all focused on how we tell our stories, not how we listen to others, or learn to shape our stories to a particular audience.

Yet obviously, communication is inherently two-way. Without listening, not only do you not know what the other person is saying, you do not know how to frame what you say to them. Listening is a critical piece of learning, and it is a huge part of building a narrative, as discussed in Chapter 13. You cannot shape a narrative unless you understand your audience.

....

EFFICIENCY

....

Once we start to consider the outbound aspects of communication, we must think about efficiency: the ability to communicate a clear and unambiguous message in the minimum number of characters, or in a limited amount of space or time.

This is important because of the growing amount of noise in a networked world. People are precious about their time and they want value from communication. Knowing how to package your message in a form that is easy to digest makes you a more attractive partner and gives you greater ability to cut through the noise.

Twitter's original 140-character limit made this a daily test for millions of people, and it is not easy. Users developed their own syntax to address the challenge. Those that were successful in the early days were the ones who best grasped this new syntax. By keeping everyone's messages short, Twitter has allowed people to scan a huge amount of information and opinion in a very short space of time. This is highly valuable in this noisy world, and the reason that so many people use Twitter as readers more than writers.

As Blaise Pascal famously said,[61] "Je n'ai fait celle-ci plus longue que parce que je n'ai pas eu le loisir de la faire plus courte." Or as it is roughly translated in English: "I'm sorry to write you such a long letter, I did not have time to make it shorter." The onus is on the writer to pare down their words – or designs – to deliver the maximum amount of content in the minimum space.

PRECISION

Precision is often lacking in workplace communication. This seems a particularly acute problem here in the UK. I wonder if this is one of the causes of our low productivity. Our manners often prevent us from being direct about what we want, meaning briefs from manager to staff, and from client to supplier, are often much woollier than they should be. Our culture means that the staff member or supplier are often unwilling to challenge the woolly brief, so instead throw themselves into the work with gusto, becoming 'busy fools' and wasting everyone's time and money.

In a 'gig economy', where the ability to brief a job clearly, and to comprehend and challenge this brief is vital, the lack of these skills will be increasingly apparent. We may see some European directness coming into our workplaces, if it is not in fact already here.

Tim Langley, my co-founder at CANDDi, a web analytics business we set up in 2009, was a fan of the phrase 'strategically lazy' to describe a communications skill he wanted to see in our staff. He wanted them to challenge briefs that lacked clarity and demand total understanding of what was expected before they would begin a task. This may sound frustrating to their managers, but he wanted to ensure that we wasted as little time as possible chasing misunderstood goals and focused our limited time and resources on tackling clearly-defined problems.

Perhaps we should teach everyone to be strategically lazy in order to increase the precision in our communications?

Train people with the skills, inculcate the practice, and give people the confidence to challenge every brief until it is crystal clear

CLARITY

Clarity too is an issue, and one that is subtly distinct from efficiency and precision. You can be precise and efficient in communication, but if the language you use is jargon-laden and complex, people must do a lot of work to comprehend it. Clarity is about lowering the mental overhead required to decode a message, because in a noisy network, people need to conserve that brain power for more important tasks.

BEAUTY

What none of these exhortations speak to though is beauty in communication. A value beyond utility that makes a piece of communication stand apart. While there is something to admire about a perfectly constructed statement, one that is clear and concise, it can always be enhanced with rhythm, poetry or wit. Adding beauty to language or design increases its power to engage and compel, excite and entertain. Signals stand out most from the noise when they are imbued with this uniquely human quality.

MANY MODES

I have written mostly about language as a medium here, but there are many modes of communication and each will have their place in tomorrow's world. Great design can obviate the need for any words at all. It is hard to foresee machines being able to incorporate all the qualities above in their visual communications to the same level of skill as a human, at least in the near future.

Within language itself there are many modes: written and spoken, one-to-one and one-to-many. As I have done more public speaking over recent years, I have learned just how different the disciplines of the after-dinner speech and the conference keynote are: both are performing to a crowd, but each requires a very different approach. The same is true of the difference between a tweet and an email, a blog post and a more formal paper. Being a truly great speaker or writer in every environment is a lifetime's work, and probably unachievable.

No one is going to master all these forms of communication. And just as I have a preference for words over design, everyone is going to have their strengths and weaknesses. What we should be doing, for ourselves and the young people who are to succeed us, is to ensure that they have at least a grounding in all of these media, and the opportunity to work out which ones they prefer. Then we need to build a curriculum, at home, at school and in the workplace, that gives them the opportunity to hone their skills.

FLYING SOLO

Just as I was finishing this chapter, I saw a tweet from the author Matt Haig. Yes, Twitter has been one of the primary distractions while I have been trying to finish this book. Haig was decrying the emphasis on teamwork as "the ultimate virtue in business, school and even creative endeavours." It struck a chord with me as what this chapter is really about is your ability to work in a team. Communication skills are your interface into a team however wide or narrowly defined. And my belief about a networked world being the natural response to the dual influences of low friction and high frequency change absolutely implies a world where we have to shout about ourselves. This worries Haig even more. As he said: "We don't want a world that ends up rewarding the people who are the most confident speakers. We want the people who are the deepest thinkers to lead us."

He may well be right. But I do not think that is the world we are going to get.

People often confuse the role of the futurist with that of the politician. Futurists like me do not usually describe the world we want to see, though we can always be persuaded, often with a beer. We spend most of our time helping people to see the world as we believe it will be, or at least a range of possibilities and probabilities.

My prescription for people to focus on the development of curation, creative and communication skills is predicated on the future I see becoming real before our eyes.

If I were to be designing an ideal future, I may well choose a different environment in which a different set of skills might be the most critical to success: systems thinking, analysis and empathy perhaps. But instead I find myself teaching my children the skills of discovery, synthesis and speaking out, because they are the people I trust most to turn the world we are likely to see into the world I would like to see.

CHAPTER 20

NEXT STEPS

At the start of this book I asked if your head was spinning. I worry that if it was not at the start, it might be now. Reading through what I have written, I realize that my intention to pare this book down and focus on just a few ideas has gone a little awry. I've ended up including quotes from German counts and Venezuelan economists. I've talked about ducks and horses, and cars and washing machines. I hope that what you have come away with is at least some level of clarity about my argument. Just in case, I will try to summarize it here.

There is a widely-shared sense of acceleration; that the world is changing faster than ever before. I reject the idea promoted by tech companies and other accelerationists that somehow the grand arc of history has moved into a higher gear. Historians make a very powerful argument that there were many periods in the past that experienced change just as dramatic as that being experienced by us today, as we go through the connected computing revolution. This is a cycle of change that started in the 1960s and probably has another 50 years to run. Just like previous industrial revolutions, it will touch every aspect of our lives, but it will take decades to fully play out. This is what I would call a low frequency change.

What the accelerationists and the historians both miss is what you might call the harmonics of this latest wave. The connected computer and the globalized economy have enabled a new type of change: high frequency change. Its cycle is measured in months or years, rather than decades. Its effects are less dramatic and not as far-reaching. But it is nonetheless impactful enough to collapse a corporation or splinter profitable chunks from its income. High frequency changes can disrupt whole sectors or industries.

We are poorly adapted to this type of change. As organizations we lack the horizon-scanning skills, decision-making abilities and corporate structures to respond to this type of change. As individuals, we are overly reliant on the longevity of the skill sets we learn in early life, and most of us have little idea of what it will take to succeed in the future.

In Part One I tried to explain the phenomenon of high frequency change. In Part Two I offered an outline of the prescription I try to bring to my clients, teaching them how to scan the near horizon, how to select and communicate responses to what they see, and how to build organizations with the agility to respond. In Part Three I suggested the skills that might inoculate us and our children from the worst effects of high frequency change, at least from a career perspective.

I hope I have achieved three things. Firstly, that I have given you an understanding of why so many of us feel like change is happening faster now, and why this sense is valid and requires a response. Secondly, that I have explained the three major components of a strategy for organizations to respond to high frequency change. And thirdly, that I have given you some pointers on how to develop your own career or the education of those young people whose lives you might influence in the face of this new phenomenon.

A CATALYST

My hope is that reading this book is not an end in itself, but rather a catalyst for action. I hope that you go back to your organization and examine its processes and structures. Are you ready for that moment when high frequency change strikes? Do you have the appropriate tools of foresight and decision-making in place to see it early, develop and act on a response? Is your organization structured in such a way that you can take radical action at the moment it is required?

If you were to take one thing back to your organization from this book, I hope it would be this: make time every six months to think about the future. Not what might happen in 20 years but what is going to happen over the next two to five years. Bring in external viewpoints to shake things up, including people from the organization who may not ordinarily have a place at the table, and voices from beyond your sector. Listen to what they have to say with an open mind. Consider the fact that you may have to radically change the direction of your organization to stay relevant.

On a personal note, I hope that this book leaves you examining your own career path and education, as well as that of your children or those young people you lead or educate. Are you teaching them the critical skills for success in tomorrow's world? Are you developing your own capabilities to enhance your own prospects?

If you were to take one, concrete piece of individual action from reading this book, I hope that you would consider taking up a new hobby. The humbling effect of starting from scratch is powerful. But really, it is about waking up the mental muscles attached to learning, remembering that there is a lot of failure involved when you start to do something for the first time, and knowing that success means learning from that failure as fast as possible and moving on.

TALKING ABOUT TOMORROW

A little over six years ago as I write this, futurism was itself a hobby. I had been writing and broadcasting about the future since 2006. First on my blog *Book of the Future*, named after the 1979 Usborne *Book of the Future*, which I was obsessed with as a child, and then on the BBC and elsewhere, where I had become recognized for my ability to explain technology stories in simple terms. A few times a week I was popping up on radio and TV to explain the latest developments in technology and trying to show what they meant for the future.

When I decided to turn the blog into a business, a friend came up with the title 'applied futurist' to capture my desire to do more than foresight, and to work on solutions as well as the problems. He also helped me design a logo and a website, something for which I am eternally grateful. Because in just a few weeks I had received calls from global corporations like LG, Nikon and Sony Pictures, all in apparent need of the skills of an applied futurist.

What I did not know then is that demand would only grow. The business of futurism has far exceeded my expectations, and though the business does not look now anything like I expected then, the need for futurists seems to be booming.

This will doubtless inspire a lot of cynicism. I confess, I fall prey to it myself when I see the explosion of people with 'futurist' appended to their job title on LinkedIn. Despite having had it as my job title for six years, it still sounds pretentious to my British ears. And I find myself questioning people's qualifications to call themselves a futurist, just as more established futurists questioned mine a few years ago. But just as I thought they should be quiet back then, I think I should now be quiet too. Because if I am right, we need more futurists.

As I hope I demonstrated in Chapter 8, most organizations are very poor at planning for the future beyond the limited scope of expanding business as usual or launching new products and services inside the current scope. We need to change the culture, behaviour and structure of our organizations to be more agile and prepared for high frequency change, and that is the role of the growing number of futurists.

Perhaps having read this book, you will add yourself to their number. Learn some tools and techniques. Become the facilitator of your organization's conversations about the future. If this idea appeals, come and find me at tom-cheesewright.com. There you will find tools you can use in your organization or career, as well as a constant supply of stories of tomorrow.

ENDNOTES

1. Frederik, Jesse. "The world's not changing faster than ever at all." *The Correspondent*, 8 April 2016. http://bit.ly/2R8gYiq

2. Cardia, Emanuela. "Household Technology: Was it the Engine of Liberation?" conference.nber.org, 10 July 2008. http://bit.ly/2S71iJm; Bowden, Sue and Offer, Avner. "Household appliances and the use of time." *Economic History Review*, November 1994. http://bit.ly/2A8GN8b

3. Warman, Matt. "Technology cuts chores to just two hours a week." *Daily Telegraph*, 8 August 2013. http://bit.ly/2S9WN0O

4. Peacock, Louisa. "Women spend half as much time on housework today compared to 1960s." *Daily Telegraph*, 5 December 2012. http://bit.ly/2R55QTf

5. The museum of English rural life, Reading University. http://bit.ly/2PQryWy

6. "Steam among the farmers." *Chambers's Journal of Popular Literature, Science and Arts*, Volumes 21-22. http://bit.ly/2PRN5OM

7. Garcia, Marisa. "What Flights Used to Cost in the 'Golden Age' of Air Travel." *Travel and Leisure*, 13 August 2017. http://bit.ly/2rMMUus

8. Pierce, David. "The weird origin story of the viral, dangerous hoverboard." *Wired*, 29 June 2015. http://bit.ly/2BvZp21

9. Hern, Alex. "'Hoverboards' are illegal on both pavements and roads, CPS confirms." *The Guardian*, 12 October 2015. http://bit.ly/2BsL2LG

10. Strange, Adario. "The rise and fall of the hoverboard." *Mashable*, http://bit.ly/2QJdR0P

11. "U.S smartphone penetration surpassed 80 percent in 2018." *Comscore*, 3 February 2017. https://bit.ly/2pT04qo

12. Desjardins, Jeff. "How Long Does It Take to Hit 50 Million Users?" *Visual Capitalist*, 8 June 2018. https://bit.ly/2Peunlr

13. Therese, Poletti. "Netflix thinks 'Fortnite' is a bigger competitor than other streaming services." *Market Watch*, 19 January 2019. https://on.mktw.net/2lGeP97

14. Anthony, Scott D, Viguerie, Patrick S, Schwartz, Evan l and Landeghem, John V. "2018 Corporate Longevity Forecast: Creative Destruction is Accelerating." *Innosight* http://bit.ly/2R461ON

15. Durden, Tyler. "4 Million Fewer Jobs: How The BLS Massively Overestimated US Job Creation." *Zero Hedge*, 5 August 2014. https://bit.ly/2UEW7pf

16. "Global Entrepreneurship Index." *The Global Entrepreneurship and Development Institute*. https://bit.ly/2vaiJic/

17. D'Arcy, Conor. "Workers on zero hours contracts hits a record high – but have they reached their peak?" *Resolution Foundation*, 3 March 2017. http://bit.ly/2Gs4sWY

18. "Freelancing in America." *Freelancers Union and Elance-oDesk*, September 2014. http://bit.ly/2SW6tMf

19. Leighton, Patricia with Brown, Duncan. "Future Working: The rise of Europe's independent professionals." http://bit.ly/2R7ecdd

20. Jackson, Mark. "EU Raise BT Competition Concern Over Business Rates for UK Fibre Broadband." *ISPReview*, 10 October 2017. http://bit.ly/2SX4cAE

21. "Regulatory sandbox." *Financial Conduct Authority*, updated 22 October 2018. http://bit.ly/2BsD3yi

22. Tide (online business bank). http://bit.ly/2CljxFA

23. "MusicNet to launch 'in 60 days'." *BBC News*, 27 September 2001. https://bbc.in/2ECy8yl

24. "Global Napster usage plummets, but new file-sharing alternatives gaining ground, reports Jupiter Media Metrix." *ComScore*, 20 July 2001. http://bit.ly/2QH3Tgk

25. Lynskey, Dorian. "How the compact disc lost its shine." *The Guardian*, 28 May 2015. http://bit.ly/2BpRwLk

26. "HMV ventures into digital waters." *BBC News*, 25 August 2005. https://bbc.in/2SSC0yC

27. "7digital Powers New Digital Music Service for HMV in Canada." *7digital*, 13 December 2013. http://bit.ly/2LpqTdV

28. Elmer-Dewitt, Philip. "How much revenue did iTunes generate for Apple last quarter?" *Fortune*, 21 July 2013. http://bit.ly/2LqAnWl

29. Robinson, Duncan. "HMV expects return to profit in 2013." *Financial Times*, 9 August 2012.

30. Ruddick, Graham. "From £2.72 a share to 2p – why HMV crashed", *The Daily Telegraph*, 16 December 2016. http://bit.ly/2SaFOeC

31. "Number of HMV stores in the United Kingdom (UK) from 2010-2017." *Statista*. http://bit.ly/2QEIxAh

32. Alm, Richard and Cox, W M. "Creative Destruction." *Econlib*. http://bit.ly/2PKVvHy

33. Ketchum, Milo S. "The design of walls, bins, and grain elevators."

34. "The National BIM Report 2018." *thenbs.com*, 10 May 2018. https://www.thenbs.com/knowledge/the-national-bim-report-2018

35. Díez, Federico J and Leigh, Daniel. "Chart of the Week: The Rise of Corporate Giants." *IMF Blog*, 6 June 2018. http://bit.ly/2ClCkAu

36. Dunn, Will. "How a new attitude to work saved Britain's bookshops." *New Statesman*, 10 July 2017. http://bit.ly/2Eyln7H; Millen, Robbie. "James Daunt: He stood up to Amazon — and saved our bookshops." *The Times*, 29 November 2018. http://bit.ly/2BupVsx

37. https://bit.ly/2UILYrJ

38. "Stevey's Google Platforms Rant." *Google+*, 12 October 2011.

39. See *Revolt on the Right* by Matthew Goodwin and Robert Ford for confirmation of both the complex nature of UKIP's support, and the importance of the men left behind in Labour heartlands to its power.

40. "Knight Frank Tenant Survey 2015/6." http://bit.ly/2PQk2uO

41. Gregg, Paul and Gardiner, Laura. "A steady job?" *Resolution Foundation*, July 2015. http://bit.ly/2EuGeIN

42. Agbonlahor, Winnie. "UK 'almost most centralised developed country', says Treasury chief." *Global Government Forum*, 27 January 2015.

43. Though most sources are just PR surveys, they all seem to reach roughly the same figure. Hope, Katie. "How long should you stay in one job?" *BBC News*, 1 February 2017. https://bbc.in/2EBu4yF

44. "Employer skills survey 2017." *Department for Education*, August 2018. http://bit.ly/2EAq2qx

45. Frey, Carl B and Osborne, Michael. "The future of employment." *Oxford Martin School*, 17 September 2013. http://bit.ly/2R9OTac

46. Graeber, David. "Bullshit jobs." http://bit.ly/2Gtvr4j

47. Arntz, Melanie, Gregory, Terry and Zierahn, Ulrich. "The Risk of Automation for Jobs in OECD Countries." *ifuturo*. http://bit.ly/2S9CqRr

48. "Putting faces to the jobs at risk of automation." *OECD*, March 2018. http://bit.ly/2rKtDKb

49. "Jobs lost, jobs gained: workforce transitions in a time of automation." *McKinsey Global Institute*, December 2017. https://mck.co/2EDHYjJ

50. "Up to 30% of existing UK jobs could be impacted by automation by early 2030s, but this should be offset by job gains elsewhere in the country." *PWC*, 24 March 2017. https://pwc.to/2EtihBL

51. "New 5th annual 'Freelancing in America' study finds that the U.S. freelance workforce, now 56.7 million people, grew 3.7 million since 2014." *Business Wire*, 31 October 2018. https://bit.ly/2QbJAnf

52. "Trends in self-employment in the UK." *Office for National Statistics*, 7 February 2018.

53. Jeffreys, Branwen. "Creative subjects being squeezed, schools tell BBC." *BBC News*, 30 January 2018. https://bbc.in/2QDjXjk

54. Richens, Francis. "GCSE results confirm drop in take-up of arts subjects." *ArtsProfessional*, 26 August 2016. http://bit.ly/2rMZNVj

55. "Facts & Figures." *Americans for the Arts*.

56. Miller, Ross. "AP's 'robot journalists' are writing their own stories now." *The Verge*, 29 January 2015. http://bit.ly/2T11dXV

57. Rhodes, Margaret. "So. Algorithms are designing chairs now." *Wired*, 3 October 2016. http://bit.ly/2PLMH48

58. "Hack Rod: Hot-rodders pioneer a new manufacturing revolution." *Autodesk*.

59. Heaven, Douglas. "The designer changing the way aircraft are built." *BBC News*, 29 November 2018. https://bbc.in/2Q3G1TP

60. Schwab, Katharine. "This AI designs Balenciaga better than Balenciaga." *Fast Company*. http://bit.ly/2A7R7gD

61. This quote has been attributed to many people, including Mark Twain and Jane Austen. It is most reliably attributed to Pascal, appearing in his *Lettres Provinciales* in 1657. See http://bit.ly/2ECweOB